Mr. & Mrs. Norman Gudersen
6273 Sunnyview
Salem, Oregon
EM 2-3019

My 3 Years Inside Russia

MY 3 YEARS INSIDE RUSSIA

by COMRADE X

As Told to . . . Ken Anderson

Based on the true story of a German soldier, taken prisoner after World War II by the Russians, and banished to Siberia

ZONDERVAN PUBLISHING HOUSE
GRAND RAPIDS, MICHIGAN

Second Printing — February, 1959

Printed in the United States of America

1

I must not tell you my name, and you will wonder why.

Please do not think it is because I am ashamed to do so, or that I am a person of note who does not wish to be made further vulnerable to the prying curiosity of the public. The fact is that I am a man of simple tastes and of humble background. You have not heard of me, and if I were to tell you my name, you would soon forget it.

You see, it is not who I am, but what has happened to me, that makes anonymity necessary. Even those of us who wish to inflict no harm upon another, who want only to live in quietness, must keep our guard lest we by a careless act bring upon others a fate they do not deserve. So, you see, it is not that we fear for our own security, but rather that we must be careful for our loved ones who have already suffered much because of us.

We live in a cruel world, across whose face there falls a deepening shadow. To those without hope, without the sure faith in a God who cannot fail, it sometimes becomes mockery to live. I have seen such faint hearts, faint though they beat in the breasts of strong men. I have watched hope die completely, and no death you have ever witnessed is so cruel as the death of hope in a living human being.

I am a German, born and raised in the Ruhr Valley. I could tell you of my childhood, of my parents and my friends, but you would find most of it commonplace. As I have already said, I stem from a humble background.

The early years of my life saw little beyond the commonplace. So perhaps it is best to begin my story in February of

1943, when I was inducted into the German *Whermacht,* the infantry of Adolph Hitler's military machine.

I remember how I went alone and poured out my heart to God. Was this His will? Was He leading me, even in this strange way, to a place of service for His glory? Or was I a slave of circumstances over which even the power of heaven had no control? God gave me peace in my heart as I prayed. It was a radiant peace, like the soft breath of evening on a Bavarian hillside. For God told me in those moments that no child of His is ever out of His sight. I had never realized that before.

Without that peace in my heart, I do not know how I could have broken the news to my dear wife. I remember how she looked at me and how the peace of God came also into her heart as it had come into mine.

"There is no choice we can make," I remember telling her, "except to resign ourselves completely into the will of God."

Due to my advanced age, so far as military requirements are concerned, I did not fight as a combat soldier, and I am grateful to God for this. I realize that in God's sight no soldier is guilty of taking a man's life. I realize, too, that although I was not in a combat unit, I contributed as much as any infantry man to the toll of lives taken from those who opposed us. Yet I am grateful to God that it did not fall my lot to engage primarily in combat warfare.

In my country, it is not everyone who drives an automobile. So the fact that I had a driver's license and had considerable experience as a civilian transporter, resulted in my being assigned to what you might call a quartermaster corps as a truck driver.

Though optimism yet dominated the scene in Germany, now we realize that the Nazi leaders — those who had not completely gone mad — read the handwriting on the horizon. Through effective propaganda, however, the severity of the situation was kept from most of the people.

So in reality, when I entered service, the dark cloud of defeat had already begun to move across Germany although few realized it. The emphasis was on defense. One seldom heard the Nazi hymn, "Today Germany is ours; tomorrow the whole world." Behind us lay the glory of the occupation of Czechoslovakia, the Polish campaign, the conquest of Norway, the Blitzkreig.

The reality of the present now was that Erwin Rommel, the Desert Fox, had been driven by the allied forces out of North Africa, a considerable blow to us German people, who considered Rommel a truly great man. Not only had the Allies conquered North Africa, but they had crept up into Italy and were expected at any moment to launch a second front across the channel from England.

Nazism still held its firm grasp upon the people and few dared to speak out against the Fuhrer and his program. I do, of course, recall those who did venture their opinions, some of whom suffered the consequences. As far as I was concerned, like so many of our people, I realized the futility of speaking my heart, so I kept quiet. I firmly believed that if Hitler was wrong, his evil would become his own destruction. For I believe with all my heart that evil destroys itself. This is not only true in the passing situations of time, but in the long expanse of eternity.

So by the time I got into the army, it was quite obvious that a good deal of the glory which had been associated with the identification of one's self to the military was gone.

As you recall, Germany's great emphasis in 1943 lay on the Russian front, where disaster threatened. The German command had believed it necessary to completely eliminate the threat of the Russian armed forces, in order that there might be freedom of action against any threat which might come from the south or the west or the north. Then, too, successful conquest of Russia would result in the acquisition of the industrial areas west of the Urals, as well as opening the way to all the supplies in the east in the rich agricultural areas of the Ukraine Donetz Basin.

So such a conquest, in addition to the elimination of the Russian military threat, would furnish materials for continuing the war over an indefinite period of time. And, needless to say, it would provide much needed morale for the German people.

Reflecting now, I sometimes wonder what would have happened had Germany brought about the defeat of Russia.

Please do not misunderstand. I did not defend, nor by any means condone, the thought of a Europe occupied by Hitlerism. But sometimes, as I sit in quiet reflection, I find myself wondering which is the larger of the two evils—Nazism or Communism? Would Nazism, if given the chance, have spread its influence world-wide as rapidly as godless Communism has done?

I personally feel that Nazism, for all its nefarious ways, was the lesser of the two evils. Surely it was least prepared for world domination. True, *bunds* could be found here and there around the world, but surely nowhere in the abundance of the Communist cells which began manifesting themselves so soon after the close of World War II.

It is all a matter of conjecture, quite beside the point now, I know. But I have wondered.

My reason for mentioning to the extent that I have the Russian campaign is that, in April of 1943, I was given the assignment of driving a supply truck to the eastern front.

A year and a half earlier, in October of 1941, the German government had announced a final drive on Moscow with the intention of ending the war by December of that year. You remember, however, that the Russian counter-attacks, which began in the Leningrad area, resulted in a considerable change of strategy. The end of December, instead of bringing victory, marked the final point of eastern advance for the German forces, necessitating a general withdrawal toward the west.

So the Russian campaign became a lethal blow, not to the Russians but to the Germans, for we never recovered from the staggering impact of that defeat. It was as though a major artery had ruptured, allowing our very life blood to drain from within us.

To prevent total disaster, the matter of getting supplies to the front became a major project. We loaded our trucks at the last railroad station and drove a distance of some forty or fifty miles to the front lines over poor roads made navigable by tree trunks laid across the deep holes that had been torn by repeated bombings. We traveled mostly at night, driving without illumination of any kind. Usually, there were ten of us in a convoy, with another convoy following just a few moments behind.

We faced constantly the threat of land mines, and you will know something of my personal anguish when I tell you that the casualty rate ran about one out of each ten trucks.

It was bitterly cold and sometimes I felt as though my hands would freeze to the steering wheel. I made many of those trips like an automaton, all but oblivious to everything transpiring about me even though at times the air was full of the flash of artillery fire and the bursting of mines and bombs.

Perhaps you have been in similar straits, constantly facing the reality that death may at any moment engulf you. Then I trust you have also experienced, as did I, the sustaining vigor of a sure confidence in the Almighty.

My parents were devout Christians, and my wife and I had endeavored to transmit the same heritage to our children. True, faith in God is a sustaining and motivating force in time of tranquillity, but how much more its recognizable value in the face of danger and uncertainty.

I am grateful for that which I have been privileged to learn of the goodness and greatness of the Lord.

2

I suppose we must await the final verdict of history to adequately delineate the character of the Russian people. At the time of World War II, Nazi leaders considered the Russians incapable of any vigorous military action. In the first place, we were told, they lacked the mental capacity for aggressive warfare. Additionally, we were assured that Communism held the people in grim servitude, and that no slave would risk his neck to save the life of his taskmaster.

Be that as it may, few soldiers have ever fought so bitterly and so gallantly as the Russians. Military pride and careful indoctrination perhaps give ample explanation for many observers as to why the Russian army was able to stop the German advance when, almost to the last man, the pledge was to die rather than surrender. Yet one wonders.

We were told in Germany that Russia was a military state and that the government had made all kinds of fantastic promises to its soldiers. To the victor belonged the spoils, they said, and the Russian soldier would receive the choicest rewards.

Yet how can one fully explain the suicidal fanaticism of the Russian soldier, who willingly threw himself into the jaws of death when the call to duty made such action necessary? What promise of earthly reward, attainable only through life, could induce him to die?

But even more difficult for me to understand was the activity of people like the Partisans. Theirs was a raw patriotism, which had no impetus other than the dictation of their own hearts.

Our greatest peril, so far as our convoys were concerned, came from the constant threat of the Partisans. Most of our route lay along wooded area, and these Partisans — not only men, but women and children — offered continual resistance from their hiding places along the dense verdure.

Was it clever propaganda which kept them faithful to the Communist cause? Or were they really faithful to Stalin at all? Could it not be that for sheer love of their own fatherland, they would not let their country fall to another, however displeased they might have been personally with the program and policies of the Kremlin?

It is true that, with the exception of Peter the Great, most Russian rulers have maintained a policy of isolation. Geographically, too, Russia's people live remotely cloistered from the rest of the world. Perhaps, like a child born blind at birth, they know only the security of whatever lot may currently befall them and must, by innate compulsion, reject any intrusion, whatever its form, imposed upon them.

I still do not know.

It was especially dangerous on the quiet nights, when the air clung about us bitterly cold and dark and still. Whenever we passed through densely wooded areas, and we constantly did, it was always with the horror of the Partisans. A hand grenade thrown into one of our cabs, the chatter of machine gun fire, a lone shot from an antiquated rifle — the impending menace was constantly there.

I remember one night as we made our way toward the front, our trucks loaded to the breaking point with supplies, particularly ammunition. We drove slowly, so slowly that I could easily have walked beside my truck, and allowed it to follow the deep, frozen ruts which had been cut by our convoys during a brief thaw a few days earlier.

We moved so slowly, in fact, that even the sound of our motors seemed but a quiet din. I was, in fact, so accustomed to the sound of those engines that they did not even register in my thinking. Instead, I heard only the ghastly silence.

We were about half way to the front, passing through a small ravine covered heavily by woods on either side, when a band of Partisans struck. First the crack of one rifle out of

9

the blackness, then another and another. The driver of our lead truck was mortally wounded and his vehicle crashed sickeningly against a fallen log alongside one edge of the ravine. It is a miracle that his ammunition did not explode and kill us all.

The tires on several of the other trucks were shot out, and the lumbering vehicles —the drivers killed or wounded — careened off to the side.

I sat petrified with fear, automatically turning my vehicle out of the path of those which had been halted by the first Partisan fire. There was nothing to do but drive forward. For the Partisans never once revealed themselves. They were like snipers, shooting long range from some hidden crows nest, so dense was the cover of timber secluding them.

It remains to this day a miracle to me but mine was one of the few trucks in our convoy which got through.

Such an awareness of God's presence came over me that night that I became almost completely insensitive to fear. *I am thy God* whispered over and over through my thoughts, quieting and assuring me.

Do not misunderstand. I did not ask God for protection while others of my comrades fell. I only trusted Him, for His will. And He gave me the deeply abiding assurance that nothing could befall me apart from His permission, nothing which would not bring glory unto Himself.

I recall another night when, apparently out of danger, we stopped briefly for rest along the road. One of our drivers foolishly ventured alone into the woods, and when he did not return after a reasonable length of time, some of our men organized a quick search for him.

We found him.

A group of Partisans had apparently followed our progress, as if in counsel with some uncanny wisdom which told them we would stop to rest, and that at least one of our member would venture into their hands, giving them a unique opportunity to spell out their hatred for the German people. Without once breaking the silence, these Russian civilians had taken our man by surprise, snuffed out his life, and then moved on into the forest leaving him hideously decapitated.

It is this one factor, above all else, that makes it impossible for me to quite understand the Russian people. Certainly it was not the sheer desire for adventure that sent these Partisans in bands, preying like hungry wolves upon our lives. Many of them were common folk, just like myself, who knew at least a measure of the peace and contentment of a common life and a happy home.

I wondered if I was ever to see my own life become like a toy in their hands.

Simultaneous with the rising tide of Russia's strength at the front, the Partisans increased their activity against us. They became so strong, in fact, that at times we found it necessary to abandon our trucks and attempt to clear known dangerous areas ahead of us before proceeding. Particularly so in one area, where we had lost a high percentage of men and trucks. Here one day, during a period when the Partisans had been particularly active, we set out to clear the way ahead of us. It was a swampy area, and our commanding officer instructed us to approach the edge of the forest through the swamps. We had to wear improvised skis to keep us from sinking into the muck.

I came upon an especially soft area, and made my way toward a clump of trees, thinking to find thereby more substantial footing.

Suddenly, a group of ravens swooped down upon me, in such a startling maneuver that I could not help but stop and turn to watch them.

I shall never cease to thank God for the miracle of those ravens, causing me to turn and look back!

For, you see, when I turned to watch the birds fly away, I saw three Partisans directly behind me, each armed with a machine gun. In another moment, they would have seen me and I would have been instantly killed. But, dropping to the earth, I was able to hide myself from view until they passed by.

Deep in my heart, the voice of God seemed to say that there was work on earth for me to do for Him, and in that silent moment, I rededicated myself to Him. It was a milestone in my life.

I suspect what you may be thinking. And I do not blame you for it. In your country, as well as in mine, no doubt there are many who, in the face of battle, make commitments to God which they fail to keep after the stress of danger has ended. Those in all parts of the earth, who only turn for divine help when they have reached the ultimate of human frailty.

God can be nothing less than Himself. We limit Him only by our unbelief. I sometimes wonder if many of those who claim to trust Him have any contact with Him at all. For He becomes no greater than their concept of Him. Doubts. Worry. Inability to commit everything to Him. These are the barriers between the believer and His God.

I make no claim to a great faith, so far as the exercises of my soul are concerned. But I can say, in complete honesty, that as I experienced the sustaining hand of my God, there grew within my heart a confidence in Him above and beyond anything I had ever dreamed possible.

I am grateful to God that He allowed my faith to be tested, for only in times of testing can one adequately measure his confidence in God.

3

Yes, war is a time when people pray.

I learned the truth of that when, after one especially perilous time near the front, I was permitted a short furlough back to my home. What a different Germany it was. As we made our way along the countryside, pockmarked by Allied bombs, it came upon me with new forcefulness the folly of man's materialistic ambitions. I realized anew that nothing short of giving to God can possibly have real meaning upon the earth.

We came through beautiful Nuremberg, certainly one of the most fascinating cities of earth. Nuremberg is a city of the arts, and of little strategic military value, and yet it had been decimated by bombings. Acres and acres of horrible rubble. One of the great museums, containing artistic treasures dating back long before the middle ages, had been cruelly blasted from the skies. Beautiful statues, broken beyond repair, jutted above the rubble. Many of the great old buildings, treasures of the past, were gone or badly damaged. Even the great castle of Nuremberg, one of the finest in the world, did not escape the fury of the skies.

It made me very sad.

I must, however, be honest in regard to the Allied bombing of churches and museums, for Germany shares in the guilt of this unfortunate situation.

Early in the war, American and British pilots carefully avoided the dropping of bombs.

A friend of mine from Ansbach told me that an American fighter-bomber flew over that beautiful town, dropping bombs on either side of the valley but completely sparing the town itself. A warning, I suppose, of the impending Allied might.

German military men took advantage of this situation and began placing radio communication transmitters in church steeples as immunity against attack.

Puzzled at their inability to silence strategic radio transmitters, U. S. military intelligence probed carefully into Germany, discovered what the Nazi leaders had done, and immediately lifted their ban on the bombing of churches and historic shrines.

Only magnificent Heidelburg completely escaped. I am told that Winston Churchill, a graduate of Heidelburg University, asked that the city be left unmarked.

But elsewhere, beautiful Germany reeled and bled under the awful impact of total carnage.

I realized that this was part of the folly of mankind. I understood — and so did many of my people, I assure you — that our country was reaping what it had sown. We had given to the world the Reformation. We had known a great faith in God. But it was my country, I must confess, where theologians first began to doubt the teachings of the Holy Bible. First they questioned the Old Testament. Then the New. And then, foolishly believing that they were setting the pattern for a new and better world of scientific reasoning, they dared to doubt the Sonship of our Lord Jesus Christ.

I had seldom been separated from my family for any prolonged length of time. So the furlough visit had a special meaning for me. My wife and I both wept as we reunited at the railroad station, and the tears flowed freely again when I came home to our children. War not only separates loved ones, but adds also the excruciating uncertainty of physical harm or death. It was a time of rest, for our city had suffered heavy bombardment and, being no longer considered strategic, had been left almost completely unmolested. So the nights were quiet and I found good rest.

It was also a time of spiritual blessing, for I learned that my dear wife had encountered experiences with God similar to mine. While I had been facing the possibility of death at the hand of Partisans, she had gone day and night under heavy aerial bombardment. At any moment, a missile could fall from the skies and inflict injury or death. In fact, one large bomb — known in America I believe as a blockbuster — fell only a few yards from our home. It did not explode. If it had, my wife and children would have been blown into the presence of their God.

"He has a purpose in leaving us upon the earth," my wife said simply. "There are so few who sincerely seek to glorify Him." I remember how she lowered her voice as she continued, for fear someone might hear and accuse her of being a traitor. "Now that it appears certain Germany has no chance of victory, people who once called upon God have turned in bitterness against Him. Such fools they are. They seem to think God is an Omnipotent Power to whom they can turn in their inconvenience, one who will bring us victory so that, in prosperity, we can go on ignoring Him as we have in the past."

I learned great lessons in the ways of God during those days at home. My wife had been much in prayer for me, the ear of her soul so sensitively tuned toward heaven that, in comparing dates, I learned she had been particularly burdened to intercede for me at God's throne during times when my life was in greatest jeopardy.

"There was this day," she said, pointing one evening to the calendar. "It was about nightfall. I received such a burden for your safety that I could do nothing but go to my room and fall upon my face before God. I cried out to Him for over an hour. Then I had peace. I knew that, whatever happened, it would be His will."

I went to my diary, and discovered that at that time I was on a convoy, moving up toward the lines. An entry in my diary said, "We encountered an exceptionally quiet night. There was no evidence of Partisans. We did not so much as hear a shot fired anywhere around us."

Do you know what I believe? I believe that, in spite of the entry in my diary, some great evil may have been hanging nearby. A danger known only to God. Perhaps someday I will know what it was. For now, I am content to thank Him for bringing to my wife's attention whatever that need might have been. I thanked God for a helpmeet so earnest in her relationship to her Heavenly Father that, at a moment's notice, she was prepared to intercede in my behalf.

You perhaps wonder about the miracle of the ravens, when — but for that miracle — my life surely would have been taken? My wife had also prayed much for me that day, having felt intensely burdened concerning my personal welfare!

How good it is to walk in fellowship with Him!

4

One of the most wonderful things about being a Christian is the fellowship we can have with believers of other countries, the realization that Christ has done in their hearts exactly the same as what He has done in your hearts — even though you have never seen each other before, though you speak a different language, though you spring from a different culture. Yet He is the same, our wonderful Lord Jesus.

Certainly nothing, from a human standpoint of view, more emphatically states the reality of the Gospel than its acceptance by the Russian people themselves. I hope that you pray for the Christians in Russia, for there are many of them. Many more than perhaps some of God's people may realize. I know they are there, for I have met them. I have had fellowship with them.

I think particularly of one time during 1943, when the German army was on the march. We came through a Russian town near Smolensk. It was Sunday morning and the sound of battle lay beyond earshot.

German soldiers were not allowed to enter civilian homes, but as I walked down one street, I heard the familiar melody of a beautiful Christian hymn. At first I looked about me for a church but, seeing none, realized the melody came from a house nearby.

Cautiously, I made my way up to the house, to the window, and looked inside. I saw some twenty people, mostly older folks. They had no chairs, so they sat upon the floor.

They continued singing for a moment, and I joined them, quietly mouthing the German words. Then, suddenly, a middle-aged man saw me.

He gave out a cry of fear. The singing stopped, and all

faces turned in muted panic to the window. I was sorry, for I had not wanted to disrupt them.

But then I brought out my Bible, and held it up for all to see. I wish you could have witnessed the joy that flooded their faces as they came and clustered about the window. I shall always cherish that time of fellowship, one of the most unusual I have ever had in my life. For even though I could not speak one word of Russian, nor they one word of German, from our hearts we all spoke to our Heavenly Father and He to us, and in Him we had spiritual communion known only to those redeemed by the blood of the Lamb.

I look forward to meeting those people in heaven!

The orthodox churches in Russia now serve as little more than museums, of historic rather than spiritual value in that they document the Russian past and, I suppose, are like sepulchers to many a young Communist — a place where religious bigotry lies buried forever.

Yet Russia does have its evangelical churches. Often unmarked, tucked away on side streets, they are nonetheless there. They are there today. And every Lord's Day, Christian people gather to worship.

It is true that not many of the young people follow the Christian faith. But there are some. We took captive prisoners of war who, upon learning that a fellow Christian was about — though even in the army of the so-called enemy — eagerly sought for fellowship, if but a few words. It may be surprising for you to learn that there were Russian soldiers who carried God's Word with them to the line of battle, even as I did.

May we never forget that God's children are everywhere! There is no curtain, be it iron or bamboo or of any other texture, which can exclude the working of God's Holy Spirit. His Book has not been destroyed, for His Word lies deeply implanted in multitudes of human hearts. And has He not promised: *My Word shall not return unto me void . . . it shall accomplish that whereunto it was sent?*

Then, too, I found God's children — my brothers in Christ

— in the Nazi Army. Never more than three or four of us at a time, it seemed, but we would get together around the Word of God. Sometimes in military barracks, if we were back behind the lines. But even in the foxholes, as they are called in some parts of the world, up near the line of battle.

We would read a few verses from the Word of God, and then share our blessings by word of mouth. There were no preachers among us. There was no chaplain. But the Lord was there, He who said: *If two or three of you be gathered together in My name, there am I in the midst of you.*

Many times when the burst of bombs hovered upon the horizon, and the cries of wounded and dying men rent the air, I stood at the very threshhold of heaven, before the throne of the Prince of Peace Himself, for I was in fellowship with those of kindred faith who looked not at the shambles of a world ruled by sin, but, instead, *for a city not made by hands, eternal in the heavens!*

Oh, there were those who scoffed at us. There were those who called us fools, who pointed us out and tried to embarrass us in the presence of our comrades. But is that not true everywhere upon the earth?

I thank God that, throughout the war, He kept in my heart the consciousness that, as I have said, His children are everywhere. Often on a starlit night, I lay stretched out, unable to sleep. And I thought of many things. Often, of course, of my wife and loved ones at home. But I thought, too, of His children . . . my brethren in Christ . . . scattered throughout the earth.

I would hear the booming of enemy fire off in the distance, and in my heart I knew that beyond the sound of that bombardment were those who, though supposedly my enemies, were in truth my brethren in Christ. I knew that in the American army, in the British army, the French army . . . that overseas in Japan, in China . . . wherever there were men, there were those who, like me, sang praises unto the Lamb worthy to be slain, the One whose blood had made the heart of a poor sinner such as myself clean enough to be acceptable in the sight of God.

5

Largely through the intervention of the United States, the back of the German army was broken before it could bring about the defeat of the Russian forces, so that 1944 saw the slow but definite German retreat on the eastern front.

I am not a man who keeps largely abreast of political affairs, for I choose rather to keep myself informed of what God is doing in the assurance that then all is well, but I understand there are many students of world affairs in the democratic world who wish American forces had not intervened in Russia, that Hitler's army had been permitted to go all the way east and bring the Soviet Union completely to her knees.

It is not for me to say.

Backward, ever backward, we made our way out of Russia and into Poland—toward the German border. Roads and streets everywhere were jammed with people in retreat.

I was assigned to one of the last units to evacuate each area. The *Spreng-Kommando* we were called, whose task it was to confiscate or destroy everything of value or strategic importance in the wake of our retreat.

Naturally, the morale of the German army dropped to its lowest ebb. Many wished that we might surrender completely, realizing that the great day of the German Reich had now come to its sunset.

"What glory is it for a soldier to die walking backward?" I heard a man mutter. "Better to surrender and live." Although he was in my platoon, I did not see him again, so perhaps he surrendered. Or perhaps he died — walking backward.

The Lord gave me much peace of heart those days, but I was also to have my testing, my time of great testing.

In November of 1944, when the German line had for a while solidified itself in western Poland, I had a day of rest from driving my truck. We were in the Polish town of Lissa and I had my first opportunity in a long while to listen to the radio.

Of all things, the news broadcast told of an air raid on the Ruhr city where my family lived. I remember how the fear stabbed deep into my heart, how I seemed to see my wife and children killed in the awful holocaust. I tried to pray, but fear stifled the utterances of my soul.

Then, next day, I received a telegram from my sister, a nurse who, because of her position, was permitted to send telegrams. Miraculously, the telegram found me.

To my horror, the message said:

Hilde und kinder am leben. Alles verloren. Klara

In English, translated: "Hilde and children living. Everything lost. (Signed) Klara."

"Lord!" I cried out from the depths of my heart. "Why? Why? Why?"

I thought of the years I had labored to build our home. It was a humble home, but my dear wife had made it a place of beauty and contentment. We were happy there, supremely happy. Now it was all destroyed. Why?

The next day, Monday, I had to drive some seven miles by way of a forest road. To gain inner strength, I stopped and went into the woods to pray. It had been snowing, and the ground lay white and cold. But that woodland solitude became a sanctuary for me.

After prayer, I asked the Lord to give me a verse of Scripture to strengthen me, which would show me that His hand was still upon me and my family. So I opened my Bible, which I had always with me, and the Lord gave me I Corinthians 12:24, the latter part of which reads *But God hath tempered the body together, having given more abundant honor to that part which lacked.* In the German translation, it reads that "God has given to the neediest the most honor."

I lifted my heart in silent, awesome gratitude to God. He was still on the throne! Why had I chafed about the loss of material things, when my dear wife and children were spared? I was both ashamed and grateful.

A few days later, I received a letter. My wife and children had gone to live in a little cabin in the woods, a place miraculously provided by the hand of God. But even more strangely, two days later I received a letter from my brother, giving that same quotation, I Corinthians 12:24, and almost the identical thoughts which had crossed through my heart in that sanctuary in the woods!

6

Backward, backward, backward, moved the vanquished German Army. The front lines no longer reached outside German territory, for during those last weeks and months of the war, early in 1945, my activity found me located largely in central Germany, so deeply had the line been driven back from its farthest point of conquest.

Morale now reached the lowest ebb, prior to all-out surrender. Many times I saw bodies of German soldiers hanging from trees, men who had been hanged for desertion.

Everywhere, roads were jammed with refugees. They were a heart-rending sight, those refugees. The ravages of war had torn most of their possessions from them and they carried their last few belongings. Such suffering and sorrow I pray God never to see again upon this earth.

One morning in the town of Fetschao, we counted ninety-seven children dead in the market square, victims of a bombing attack the previous night. Have you ever seen so many mothers standing at the sight of their dead children, their hearts broken beyond tears, wailing out the agony of their very souls? I wish the men of this world who make war, those who whether openly or secretly draw their plans with battle lines . . . I wish they could have been there. For it is hard for me to believe that there lives a human heart who could have remained unmoved at so terrible a sight.

The nature of all activity changed considerably now. Instead of hauling supplies to the front, I engaged in carrying supplies back to the rear positions. Although I am not a military man, the futility of it all became impressed strongly upon me. Why did we try to hold out? What point was there in standing against the onrushing tide of the enemy? Yes, I loved my country. If you have ever seen Germany, the classic beauty of her country-sides and the fine majesty of her cities, you can understand my feeling. Ours is a great country. And I would not hestitate to defend her honor. But there is neither sense nor reason in war, believe me, no matter who be the victor or the vanquished. I have never waged combat for a victorious army, but I am sure that among just men, even in victory the spoils of war have an acrid smell. For how can one, whoever he may be and whatever his cause, be proud of having laid cities waste, of having plumented thousands of lives into eternity, of having ruined art treasures, marred countrysides, and left fertile farmlands desolate?

So it was not only the fact of impending defeat which weighed heavily upon me those days. No, not even the fact that as we moved backward, we came upon example after example of ravaged cities and pillaged countrysides. It was just the total meaninglessness of war that came upon me, the awful fact that here was unregenerate man trying to solve his problems without the guidance of Almighty God. Night after night, as I lay down to sleep, it was to pray with John of the Apocalypse, *"Even so, come Lord Jesus."* Only He, the glorious Prince of Peace, can ever bring meaning to this world of ours! He, who alone can heal the torn hearts of wayward men, holds the only solution to the total depravity of a lost mankind!

Certainly it must be said, for the most part, the German soldier lost the will to resist. True, there were fanatical segments who tried to maintain aggressive fronts. But the home-loving German soldier, the one who would face the facts and think, saw the futility of it all and hoped, at best, for an honorable peace which would permit him to return to his loved ones.

Time and again reports sifted through to us that the Government officials were negotiating with the Allies for a surrender. When such reports came through, hope would brighten the faces of many of us. But always, orders came through that we were to continue the resistance. Hitler and his henchmen were not giving up the fight.

"Do not be afraid," we were told again and again. "*Der Furher* has one final stroke of military genius which may yet bring the enemy to its knees."

There was much discussion about this. Was it some secret weapon? Was it a new bomb, a devastating poisonous gas, some other fantastic invention? Frankly, few of us put any stock in the reports. And so, while we presumed to be continuing our aggressive tactics against the enemy, we day by day became more passive in our resistance, and hour by hour longed for the moment of cease fire.

During these last days of the war, and the impending total doom of our country, it became continually more easy to witness for my Lord. Yes, some were afraid. It is always true, as someone among the Allies said, that there are "no atheists in foxholes." I think we Germans can add that there "are no atheists among retreating battalions."

But it was more than fear that impelled men to turn their hearts heavenward. It was the realization of the utter futility of what we had been doing, of the complete hopelessness war brings upon all those who participate in it.

I thanked God time and again for the opportunities I had to bear witness to my Saviour. For it is a serious thing to be one of His spokesmen upon this earth. Having identified oneself as a Christian, one can expect to have others, who know not the Lord, single him out for help in time of need. Such was often my experience during these final days.

"How can you speak of faith in God when the death rattle is even now in the throat of our fatherland?" one bitterly disillusioned young man asked me. In our further conversation, I found him to be a graduate of Erlanger, a man with a brilliant mind.

"Faith in God has nothing to do, for its basis, with the passing whims of our mortal lives," I told him. "So long as mankind remains alien to God, there will come war and heartache to the earth. How else can it be? The Bible tells us *evil men and seducers shall wax worse and worse.* It also says, *The heart of man is deceitful above all things, and desperately wicked.* What else can one expect in such a world?

"Someday, I firmly believe, Jesus Christ shall come to bring peace to the world. But while the world awaits that coming, He offers peace individually to any man who will trust Him."

"How do I trust Him?" the young man asked, and I saw his heart opening like a bloom in the warm bask of the spring sun.

"By faith," was my reply. "Recognize yourself to be a sinner. *All have sinned and come short of the glory of God.* But realize, also, that *Christ died for our sins, according to the Scriptures.* For, my good friend, the Bible clearly reveals that *Christ Jesus came into the world to save sinners.* And simply by trusting in His finished work, you may be saved. *Whosoever shall call upon the name of the Lord shall be saved.* You realize yourself to be totally lost without Him, like a drowning man, and you call out to Him to save you!"

Ah, there is much of this world's wisdom unknown to me. But this I know. The greatest military victory on earth fades into nothing when compared to the triumph of seeing one soul snatched from the brands of hell and set surefooted on the road to heaven!

7

I shall never forget April the 27th, 1945.

The backward motion of our retreat had taken us into the general area of Berlin. Confusion held sway everywhere, in spite of the high command order that Berlin must be defended at all costs. My unit, almost totally without supplies, could do little in the way of resistance. Further retreat was not possible, since all bridges leading to western Germany had been destroyed. We could only offer token resistance, then await capture.

I was in the suburb Berlin-Nethlitz near world-famous Potsdom. The great *Wehrmacht Kaserne,* a huge supply camp, had been located here during the war. Now, however, the staff of this camp had fled, leaving no one in command.

Together with a comrade, I secured a brand new outfit, complete from boots to cap. We also made our way into the food rations area and, desperately hungry, feasted like kings for a few moments. There was no thought of doing wrong, since everyone now knew that the cause was lost, that it would be only a matter of days, perhaps hours, until all of Germany must fall.

After we had eaten our fill, we found a rucksack and filled it with such foodstuffs as bacon, bread and army rations. Earlier that day, prior to our escapade in the supply area, we had been told by our commanding officer, a colonel, to fight to the utmost. Then, only a short while later, we watched him commandeer one of the few remaining *Wehrmacht* vehicles and leave us to retreat.

I said to a comrade, "We're without leadership. The war is over for us. There is no sense in trying to remain here.

We may as well attempt to retreat and lose ourselves in the throngs."

Fighting seemed the more useless when I realized that the Russian unit pressing against us consisted mainly of women. They were dressed like men, had short-cut hair, and a demoniac thirst for the kill. None of us wanted to shoot at them, but it was a question of personal survival. It was impressed upon me the more strongly how strange and horrible are the ways of war.

Not only did the Russians have units of women soldiers, I might add, but there were also children's battalions, youngsters no more than ten to twelve years of age. You can understand that "decent" fighting was no longer possible.

My comrade and I destroyed our weapons and tried to dig a shelter in the fenced-in garden of a house. There we lay, from about ten o'clock in the morning until noon, listening to the constant drone of artillery fire, leaving no doubt that the enemy pressed even closer, making imminent the hour of our capture.

Suddenly, a bomb burst nearby, and my friend cried out in pain.

"I've been hit!" he screamed above the din.

I could only lie motionless for a moment, wondering if I too might have been a victim of the explosion. Then, slowly, I lifted my head and looked. To my relief, I found that no bomb fragments had entered our foxhole. Rather, a brick had fallen from a building nearby and had struck my friend on the leg inflicting only a surface wound.

I had become numbed by the unreality all about me, and I think it was about eleven thirty that morning before I thought to pray.

"Lord," I remember the words of my prayer clearly, "I put myself completely into Thy hands. I am Thy child. Now, please, kind Lord, give me something from Thy word to succor me in these the direst moments of my life."

In majestic lovingkindness, the Lord gave me verses nine through thirteen of Psalm 56, which read: . . . *God is with me, In God will I praise His Word: In the Lord will I praise His Word. In God have I put my trust: I will not be afraid what man can do unto me. Thy vows are upon me, O God: I will render praises unto Thee. For Thou hast delivered my soul from death: Wilt not Thou deliver my feet from falling, that I may walk before God in the light of the living?*

Moments later, a Russian soldier approached the house near which we had dug our hiding place. Almost as soon as we saw him, he saw us. I looked at my comrade and he looked at me, and for one moment neither of us moved. Then, almost in unison, we raised our arms in surrender.

Brusquely, the Russian motioned for us to come to him, and we obeyed.

Fear struck deep into my heart, but then the words of the Psalm came to me. *In God have I put my trust: I will not be afraid what man can do unto me.* Deep in my heart, I praised God for His Word and for the ministration that Word had given me at this hour of my great need. And I was ashamed, ashamed of my unbelief, of my slowness to trust the God of Heaven who, I was convinced, saw every move I made and was mindful not only of my present plight but of the future which lay ahead.

A new sense of peace came into my heart.

The soldier quickly searched us for weapons and, finding none, bluntly took my watch, my friend's watch and wedding ring. He took my rucksack and examined it momentarily. Then, muttering something in Russian, gave it back to me and motioned for us to move to a nearby clearing. The clearing opened onto a farmyard and here we found nine other German prisoners of war with two Russian soldiers. We were led behind a barn and permitted to sit down on some fallen tree trunks.

Together with the nine other captives was an aged fireman — he must have been seventy — who had been taken captive because he wore a uniform.

We did not speak as we sat there, the sound of battle

somewhat lessened by the stone wall of the old barn. Nor did we speak as we saw the Russian soldiers move about the barnyard, taking anything which caught their fancy. They made a make-shift meal of eggs and chicken, food which seemed to be quite a luxury to them.

One of the soldiers, a very young lad, seemed arrogantly proud of his role as captor. He came up to us and stood, hands on his hips, staring at us. He said something in Russian but, of course, neither of us could understand him. Then, as though he were afraid to taunt anyone whose strength might be greater than his, he went up to the old man, the fireman. Waving his arms, he shrieked something in his own tongue.

The old man looked up at him, shook his head.

Once more the young Russian shrieked out a command in his own tongue, and once more the old man shook his head, trying to convey to the lad that he could not understand.

Suddenly, without warning, the lad struck the old man in the face. I was shocked, and arose to resist, but my comrade pulled me back down. The young man struck again and again, and the more the old man cried for mercy, the more the boy taunted him.

Once more, I started to my feet in opposition, and again my comrade pulled me down. "Be careful," he whispered. "They are wild now at the realization of victory. They hate us. We must not offer the slightest provocation, where it could mean our lives."

I'm not sure what the outcome might have been, had not a Russian officer come up from the road to us. At sight of him, the young upstart disappeared.

"*Paschly!*" the officer shouted. I would soon learn the meaning of that word, to "hurry up."

We marched for some thirty minutes, until we reached a field where about two thousand German soldiers were held captive. The feeling of relief came upon me now, for I felt that at least we were not in danger of any sudden execution on the part of any young fanatic.

It was a strange feeling, marching as a captive. To look out upon familiar countryside, familiar landmarks, and yet to be as one in a strange and distant place.

It was the beginning of a long, long parenthesis in my life.

8

While it was true that disorganization had come to the German army, there was also only the semblance of order on the part of the Russians. Victory seemed to have come more quickly than they had anticipated, and it was apparent that they were making policies and instituting their program of handling the situation on a moment-by-moment basis.

They searched our possessions for anything that might be of value to them, and confiscated freely. I thanked God that it was the spring of the year, not fall or winter, when they took our felt boots from us. They seemed to be especially anxious for good footwear.

Having participated in the well-organized and excellently outfitted Germany army, it was difficult for me to become accustomed to the fact that the Russians wore no rank insignia on their uniforms. The cut and color of the uniforms varied, too, and officers could often be differentiated only by the fact that some of them were dressed a bit better than the general run of soldier.

We wondered at times if the Russians might be trying to hide from us the fact that they, too, found themselves in a state of confusion, for they led us three days into various parts of Berlin. At times we would come near areas where last-ditch fighting remained in progress and would be abruptly ordered to do an about-face and head in the direction from which we had come. We received no food, very little water, and some of the German prisoners, already weakened, fell to the ground. I do not know what happened to them.

I want to be fair in any mention of the Russian people. It is one of the unfortunate attributes of war that one always thinks of the enemy in terms of total depravity. While it is true that a smoldering hatred has long existed between the German people and the Russian people, I certainly want to emphasize that, at least on the part of German Christians, there is the same love for all men that exists in the hearts of God's children everywhere. I am, of course, aware of the nefarious record history has recorded regarding the conduct of some parts of the German army. I am equally aware of the conduct of the Russians. But I must be honest and say that I met very many wonderful Russian people, and I saw kindness even those first days among members of the Russian army.

Some of them would show us pictures of their loved ones back home in Russia and would look with great interest as we shared photographs of those dear to our hearts. One soldier, who could speak a smattering of German, shook his head sadly. "It is too bad that you cannot return to your people," he said. "It is too bad."

I think one of the things which ameliorated the attitude of some of the Russian soldiers was the fact that they discovered the falsity of Communist propaganda regarding the way of life of the German people. Since Germany had been depicted as a capitalistic country, propagandists had pictured the life of the German people — specifically the capitalists, that is — as that of ease and splendor. The working man, the people were told, lived a life of abject squalor.

So the Russians were surprised to find the way of life of working people in a capitalistic country. One Russian soldier was reported to have said, "When my unit entered the suburbs of Berlin, we saw beautiful homes and well-tended gardens. We decided that it was a suburb occupied by rich capitalists, and began to loot and burn, only to discover that we were actually in a working class district." Asked by an

30

American if that stopped the plundering, the Russian said, "No, but I've had a lot of thinking to do since then."

To try to combat what was happening to the Russian soldiers, an army newspaper edition of *Red Star* began a propaganda attack against the "false glitter" of life under capitalism. One of its articles said, "We must pass through foreign countries. A lot of gaudy tinsel will blind your eyes. Comrades, do not believe the deceitful nightmares of a pseudo-civilization!"

The story is told of one Red soldier who held up a German and demanded his watch. "But I have no watch," the German said. "I am a poor worker and never could afford one." Thereupon the Russian soldier took one of the watches out of his bulging pocket, which was full of loot he had taken from other Germans, and said, "Take it, victim of capitalism, and thank the Soviet Regime!"

After three days, we were headed in an eastern direction out of Berlin. Traveling completely on foot, we passed through eastern Germany and into Poland. We had almost nothing to eat and it was difficult going. At night, we stopped in empty houses or other large buildings which had been left dormant in the wake of war. Carefully, I rationed out the remaining provisions in my rucksack and thanked Almighty God from the bottom of my heart.

Each morning, we were lined up for roll call and there were always many missing — some who had escaped, but more often those who had committed suicide during the night. In the course of our eastward march, however, our number increased to nearly ten thousand prisoners, by the addition of captives taken in areas along the way.

The countryside was almost ghost-like, as we made our journey. We met few civilians, and villages and farms alike stood gaunt and inanimate. It was spring and already the grass and the trees had sprung out in verdant glory, endeavoring to hide the pockmarks of the winter's warring.

We met few civilians — few living civilians, I should say — for along the road as we traveled we saw many, many unburied dead, many lying naked, their bodies having been stripped of all usable clothing and personal possessions. Plundered suitcases and carriages cluttered many areas of the road. We passed battle areas, too, where I had participated as a soldier only a few weeks or months earlier.

It was a strange and terrifying experience.

At the sight of so many human bodies, many in the state of advanced decomposition, Russian and German soldiers alike experienced violent seizures of nausea. Particularly painful, I learned, when one has had little or no food.

Perhaps nothing depresses the human spirit more than the sight of carnage and the utter silence of war's aftermath. Bombed buildings. Destroyed villages. Dynamited bridges. Mortar shells. And human bodies. All this reminiscent of the days and nights and weeks and months of almost constant warfare. Droning of planes overhead, shrieking and cursing and all that makes for the noise of war. And now, now nothing but silence. Silence broken only by the steady clump, clump, clump of our marching feet. Or perhaps the faint song of some bird that had ventured back onto terrain from which all of its kind had been blasted away the previous summer.

I am not a pacifist, in the strictest sense of the word. Did I not serve in the German army? But this I know. As a human being who wants to live his life decently, as one who claims to know the Lord Jesus Christ as his personal Saviour and Lord, I can only say that war is horrible. All that is evil in man, all that is evil in the world, comes into sharpest definition during periods of war.

Many times the sights about me became so distressing that I would lift my eyes heavenward and search the clean, cloud-washed blue of the sky overhead. Here was the only true meaning to life, the human heart with explicit faith in God. I thanked God for a *weltenschaung* that gave me ballast in so confused and wicked a world, for an enduring faith in the one who said, "*In the world ye shall suffer tribulation. Be of good courage, I have overcome the world.*" I had had times of deep spiritual experience as a civilian, even more as a soldier in training, and still more while out on the field, but now my faith in God and what it meant to me came into the fullest realization I had ever known. I could lower my eyes from the sky. I could face the reality of a destroyed Germany all about me. I could look into the eyes of my captors, and face the completely unpredictable future which lay ahead of me. I could do all this, and be a man at peace.

So great, so very great, is the power of God in the lives of those who dare to trust Him!

9

Day after day, traveling always by foot, we moved toward the Russian border. We received no allotment of food, being expected to forage along the way. Fortunately, I still had some provender in my rucksack, enough to maintain subsistence strength, and I thanked God, for on many days I would have had nothing else.

In each house, where we would find shelter for the night, German soldiers desperately sought for something to eat. In addition to hunger, many suffered from dystrophy, derived from inadequate water supply. Earnestly, I asked God to give me physical strength, to keep me free from sickness, and He graciously answered my prayer. I had a strange feeling of destiny — from my soul's innermost recess a conviction that God was going to use me for His glory through this dire state of affairs which had come into my life. I would not bequeath my plight upon anyone else, far be it from that, but I do wish that others of my Christian friends across the world could know the peace that came when, so desperately needing God's help, I placed my trust completely in Him.

For, those days, He taught me to trust. He showed me that

prayer is simply worship and trusting — worship for the one who is greater than all circumstances, trust in His implicit care and wisdom.

I did not ask God for miracles. I did not ask Him to set me free. I only trusted Him, implicitly, believing that all things do work together for good to those who love Him, content to know that He who watched the sparrow had his eye on me, and that He was going to make it possible for me to glorify His name.

On May 6th, we arrived at Landsberg, a very large camp. Here we received our first meal, and I thanked God, for my private supply of nutrition had been exhausted.

The Russians set up a tonsorial production line, and everyone of us got his hair cut. To the very skull, until we looked like a motley crowd indeed.

At first we thought the purpose of this was to more clearly identify us as prisoners, once we entered Russia. And I suppose this may have in part been the case, but I overheard a medical corpsman nearby explain to one of our men that it was to avoid possible contamination by lice.

"Are they admitting that the Soviet Union is over-ridden by fleas?" someone muttered, when the official left.

But no one laughed. No one felt like laughing.

Following a short stay at Landsberg, we moved onward. Walking. Always walking. From early morning until late at night. Often, sick and exhausted, men would fall at the wayside.

And there was no mercy.

Lord, I prayed, *I trust thee. Whatever comes, I trust Thee. Be Thou everything to me. Everything, Lord.*

And my heart was at peace.

We crossed the Polish border, arriving on the twelfth of May at Posen. Many of us had had to look for landmines, a dangerous work, but for the most part there were no incidents. Many of the men didn't care anyway, almost preferring to be blown to bits by an explosion to their present plight.

For some reason, the Russians became more free in their attitudes as we progressed nearer their home soil. They had been stiff and formal before, and while they did not now show any especially friendly spirit, they seemed more human, lessening our fears of mistreatment.

It was at Posen that we got our first introduction to *kasch,* which would be standard fare for us in the months to come. *Kasch,* a Russian staple, is some sort of tasteless oat cereal. I presume that it was more tasteless than normal, being served to prisoners of war, although, of course, I have never had occasion to eat it when prepared as anything approaching a delicacy.

We also received the first of several de-licings. I was grateful for this, since we were to be subjected, and had been, to accommodations far from sanitary, so tightly housed on many nights that breathing became next to impossible. Such a common thing as warm water, which one would take for granted, became a luxury to be dreamed about in the restless, cold darkness.

As might be expected of any conquering army, I suppose, the Russians had confiscated all sorts of items in their pathway.

One of our guards had a pocket full of watches and clocks. One of the clocks suddenly began to ring and he madly tore the timepiece out of his pocket, threw it to the ground and then, stepping off at a safe distance, shot it to bits with his pistol.

Apparently he had never seen an alarm clock before.

Posen was, in a very real sense, the beginning of our long imprisonment, with each German carefully checked, interrogated and assigned. Little of this information was, of course, shared with us, but it became quite obvious that our destinies were being charted.

"What will they do with us?" one young man asked me, terror flaming from deep within his eyes.

"We are prisoners of war," I said, "and I presume we will be taken to a camp."

"But I have heard of the Russian camps," he said. He looked about him, to make sure no guard heard his words, although since he spoke German and few of the rank and file of the Russian army knew our language, he need not have feared. "They will starve us to death," he said.

Another captive, nearer my age, had overheard and mumbled, "They will more likely work us to death." He did not lift his eyes from the ground as he spoke, and gave no indication of having participated in our discussion.

"I am very greatly frightened," the young man said. "I wish there was some way to escape."

I took my Bible from my rucksack. "There is no need to fear," I said. "Let me tell you of the peace that I have found for my own heart."

He stared at me for a moment, then at the Book, then back at me again. At first, I thought perhaps it was a spiritual hunger I saw in his eyes.

But then he said, "Do not speak to me of that Book!"

"Why?" I asked.

"I was one of the Hitler Youths," he said. "I was taught the truth about the Bible, about what it really is. Why should I change now? Why should I become a coward, when fate is turned against me?"

"But you said you were afraid," I reminded him.

His face flushed, "Aren't you afraid?" he asked. A sneer curled his lips upward.

"Except for the Word of God," I said, "I would know fear even greater than yours."

I tried earnestly to press the issue, but he would not speak to me further. Instead, he got up and moved as far away as he could without attracting the attention of one of the Russian guards.

The next morning, before we left Posen, they found him dead. He had slashed his wrists in the night with a jagged piece of glass he had found upon the ground.

My heart was greatly saddened.

This man was only one of the many who, unable to face

the uncertainty of the future, took their lives. It gave me a sense of great urgency, a keen desire to make known what Christ had done for me, to set at peace — with His peace — the hearts of those who were troubled.

I was able to bear witness to some, but there was so little opportunity. Anyone who moved at any abnormal degree about the encampment, or who even tried to gather any of the prisoners about for discussion, was severely reprimanded. Not that I feared what might befall me, should I boldly proclaim my faith in Christ, but I felt that my duty was to remain ever alert to the guidance of the Holy Spirit as to those to whom I might witness. If God had made it clear to me that I should raise my voice and endeavor to proclaim Christ, at the possible expense of my own life, I would have done so, but I did not feel this to be His leading; I felt, instead, that He had a longer term of service for me.

I prayed earnestly that He would send to me those who needed the strength of my witness, and day after day saw my prayers answered.

I repeat once again the expression, "There are no atheists in foxholes." Well, I did not find many atheists in prison camps, either. But, nonetheless, I recognized the fact that under the impulse of fear, men might assume a commitment to Christ which, in reality, became nothing more than a grasping attempt to find some kind of stability for the flesh rather than for the spirit.

I do believe, however, and give praise to God for this confidence, that I shall someday meet in heaven those whom He permitted me to reach with the message of salvation.

One former German officer, who slept on the ground near me, had a bitter spirit. He spoke constantly of his exploits during the war and pointed out repeatedly and in considerable detail what he believed to have been the fallacies of the German High Command resulting in Germany's humiliation.

"Defeat should never have been necessary," he insisted. "We could easily have won. But the High Command was stupid. There was not a brain among them. They followed the old guard ideas. They had no imagination with which to fully utilize modern methods of warfare."

Then he would lapse into a voluminous exposition of how, given the authority, he could have turned defeat into victory. Even after the opening of the second front and the withdrawal in the east.

I think perhaps I would not have spoken to him, had it not been for the fact that he was most blasphemous, cursing God with nearly every other word coming out of his mouth.

"My friend," I said, in the still of the night when I was able to speak with him alone, "this is a difficult time for all of us. I was not an officer in the army. I was only an ordinary soldier. But if you will permit me, I can tell you how you can see all of this in a tolerable light."

He turned to me and in the darkness I could not quite make out the attitude of his countenance.

I said, "Germany is no different from all the other nations of earth. We have all become sufficient in ourselves, turning our backs upon God and His rightful place in our lives and our homes and our communities. Have you ever thought that God may have given you a great privilege in permitting you to be subjected to this experience?"

"You talk like a fool!" he mumbled.

"Are you sure?" I asked, sensing the confidence of my faith in every word I spoke.

He kept silent.

"If you will permit Him to do so, God can show you through this experience the total folly of materialism." Then, quoting verse after verse of the Bible from memory, I pointed out to him the fact that all men are sinners, having nothing of divine merit in themselves, that it is the natural bent for men to seek the riches and the pomp of this world. And then I pointed him to Christ, the Lamb of God who came to take away the sin of the world, the One in whom only we can find peace and satisfaction, whatever fabric the fates may spin for us.

When I stopped speaking, he was sobbing softly.

"You speak as my mother used to speak," he said, and he was so different now. "I broke her heart."

"She is gone?" I asked.

"Yes. We lived near Heidelberg, and she was killed in one of the bombings. I wanted her to move into Heidelberg, as I had heard that Winston Churchill, who attended the University, had asked that no bombs be dropped upon that city. And no bombs were ever dropped there, but my mother did not move. She was needed where she was."

The night hung heavy with silence, and I waited. Several men, hearing our conversation, had elbowed over to us. They waited, too, like the audience at the first performance of an intense drama. As, indeed, it was.

"She talked as you talked," he continued, "but I did not heed her. I fell into much sin. As a boy and in the army."

Again there came silence, and again I waited.

"My mother . . . the last time I saw her . . . said she would pray God to send someone across my path who could bring me to see my need of the Saviour. This is the answer to her prayers."

"You would want some day to see your mother again?" I asked.

He nodded. "If only to ask her forgiveness," he said.

"But you can do much more than that," I told him. "You can enjoy with her the glory of redemption for all eternity. And by trusting now in her Saviour, by making Him your Saviour, you can so prepare your life that, when your time comes to join her, you will also be able to present to the Lord a life lived in unselfish dedication to Him."

"I want that," he said. "I have lived a sham for years. Deep in my heart, I have longed for my mother's faith, but I did not have the courage to stand for Christ."

"It will take courage to stand for Him now," I cautioned. "But if you seek it, He will give you strength."

"I will stand for Him," he said.

And there on the ground, there in the stillness of the night, there as a captive of the greatest Communist nation of earth, I pointed this wayward soul to Jesus Christ.

Long after he had fallen asleep, I lay searching the heavens. Seldom had the Lord seemed more near to me. Or my confidence in Him more secure.

I prayed that night for my wife and family. For my other loved ones. Somehow, I felt that it would be a long, long, time until I saw them again, if ever. Yet I knew, as surely as I knew my name, that God had made no mistake in placing me here. I was one of His chosen ones and, by His help, I would serve Him faithfully.

It was not easy, knowing my family needed me to re-establish our home which had been decimated by the bombings. What would my wife do for food and clothing and shelter? Who would look after her? I could only leave everything in the Heavenly Father's care!

10

At Posen, we were loaded onto freight cars, destined for Russia. European freight cars are only one-half to two-thirds the size of American cars, so you get something of an idea as to travel conditions when I tell you that ninety-three men were placed in each car.

From May 12th through 19th, we were completely locked in. Even the air register was closed. We had to drill holes in the floor to provide a means for the disposal of excrement. Our route, I later learned, was to take us through Kutno, Warschau, Brest and Borosnow, ever eastward toward our initial destination, Moscow.

While I do not believe that I suffered more than normal claustrophobia, there came times when I suffered from great depression — confined, as in a tomb, within the boxcar. Several of the men in our group lost their nerve completely and had to be subdued by fellow-prisoners lest they inflict not only harm upon themselves but upon others as well. We knew neither night nor day but for the cracks in the sides of the car and the holes we ourselves had bored in the floor. That, plus the occasional opening of the door to give us the most meager of food rations, usually late at night.

An intensely bright light would be shown into the car, when the food was brought at night, and had anyone tried to escape, he would have had to do so in full view of Russian guards. That became very apparent on the first night when, on seeing the door open, one man attempted to leap for safety. I am quite sure that machine gun bullets began riddling his body before he so much as struck the ground!

I could not hold malice toward our captors for this. We were prisoners. We were subjected to the decisions of those who had taken us prisoners. If we attempted to thwart those decisions, it was ours to suffer the consequences.

Then one day, when it seemed our lot would become totally unbearable, for we had been confined to the boxcar exactly a week, the train pulled onto a siding in a rural area. The guards ordered us to get outside. It felt good, for the air was brisk, and I filled my lungs again and again.

"Where are we?" I asked a man next to me.

"Russia," he said.

"How do you know?" I asked.

He glanced at me for a moment, shrugged his shoulders, then replied, "Where else could we be, having traveled always eastward for such a long time?"

He was correct, for, after we had been brought to attention, a Russian officer addressed us in understandable German saying, "You are in the Soviet Union. It is now increasingly important that, as the wards of our goverment, you conduct yourself properly at all times." He spoke in an almost friendly tone, as though he were trying to reason with us. "You can understand," he continued, "how careful we must now be about escapees. You shall be watched with the greatest of alertness at all times. It is to your personal advantage that you conduct yourselves appropriately."

We were compelled to remove all of our clothes. We could only keep that which we could carry in one hand and, since it appeared quite definite we would not be traveling at least in this train any longer, I took my dufflebag with me.

It was embarrassing, being subjected to nudity in the open like this. And it was cold, as we marched along an open road, toward a barbed wire enclosure, I thought of the months in the past when I had been in Russia, not as one of the conquered ones, but as a member of an army that fully intended to become the conqueror. I remembered, as the chill now moved in upon us, how cold it had been late into the spring. Even now, in the month of May, it was cold.

But my embarrassment reached its greatest height when, having reached the barbed enclosure, several members of the Russian medical corp, all of them young women under twenty years of age, came to examine us. I kept myself covered as best I could with the aid of my dufflebag. Two of the girls, working nearby, noticed my embarrassment and laughed at me. But they did not subject me to humiliation other than that.

A number of the men in our contingent had become very weak and ill and they were sorted to one side. I do not know what happened to them. The rest of us, the majority, were led to a place where the Russians issued old and badly-worn *Wehrmacht* uniforms, plus equally dilapitated accessories.

"Why is this?" I heard a comrade ask. "Why didn't they let us keep the uniforms that we had when we were captured?"

"They want us to look as defeated as possible," another man said. "We are to be marched on exhibition in Moscow."

"Where do you get that information?" he was asked.

"One of the men in our group understands Russian," he said. "He heard two of the officers talking."

We were not issued any shoes, and all of us dreaded the thought of additional marching. In this area of Russia, snow yet lay on the ground in some deeply shaded places, it was that cold.

We marched several miles to another railroad area where we were again loaded onto a train. Why we had to march to this place, instead of being taken there by train, I do not know. Perhaps it was to facilitate the movements of prisoners in some way.

These trains were more habitable, however. At least the one I rode had openings so that we could breathe more freely. It was cold, but I preferred the discomfort of spring chill to near-suffocation.

11

Our next destination was Wyschni-Woltschek, northwest of Moscow. Here we again detrained, and this time the entire group was examined by a Jewish doctor who diagnosed the total health of the prisoners as very poor. He prescribed a day of rest, welcome news to all of us.

I wondered how some of our group must have felt, those who perhaps had been caught in the wave of anti-Semitism that swept Germany prior to and during the war. For it was quite obvious that this doctor, realizing our plight, had shown us mercy.

I slept almost that entire day and on into the night.

By this time, I keenly sensed the toll that had been taken upon my body during the past weeks. Lack of sleep, insufficient diet and the constant presence of poor sanitation had left me very weak. I sensed a swelling in my legs, an indication that I might be at least mildly afflicted with the dread dystrophy.

Lord, I remember praying, *if it be Thy will, permit me to*

*have sufficient health so that I can endure whatever lies
ahead, and so that I shall have strength with which to bear
witness for Thy name.*

And even as I prayed, I asked God to search my motives,
lest I be asking that which would be only for my own con-
venience. More than any time in my life, I was in the heart
of the refiner's fire. I found myself constantly searching my
thoughts, the innermost recesses of my heart, lest there be
anything that would hinder the effectiveness of my witness.

I think nothing so warmed my heart as the fact that God
permitted me to hold no malice toward the Russians. Surely
that must be the trademark of our lives, if we do seek earnestly to walk rightly with our Lord. Love for all men, be
they friend or foe. Some of our men, obviously desiring fa-
voritisms, exhibited an obsequious spirit. The Russians detected that and often imposed the greatest hardships upon
those who so conducted themselves. For some reason, surely
it was the grace of God, they detected the fact that I wanted
to be sincere in my attitude toward them. I did not receive
what you would call preferential treatment, but neither was
I subjected to many of the inconveniences which befell the
lot of others.

Yet, believe me, it was for no thought of personal gain
that this warmth had come to my heart. God had shed there,
through His Holy Spirit, the love of Christ. If my Saviour,
hanging upon a Cross with the weight of mankind's total
sin upon His body, could cry out His love to a lost world,
saying, "Father, forgive them!", then, surely, I, who was
caught merely in circumstances of the fruits of war, could
surmount the bitterness that was expected of me and, instead,
see all men as those for whom Christ died.

Following our day of rest, we were given blue cotton sacks,
and instructed to march to an area where we would find
straw with which to make mattresses.

I was happy at this, for it had been difficult sleeping on
the hard floor of the boxcar and I supposed that there would
be much more traveling by train.

We were not fortunate as we had hoped, however, as the hay which we went to get was for the officers watching over us. But after we had supplied mattresses for the Russian officers, we were given rough burlap sacks and, under the most careful surveillance, taken to a wooded area where we were permitted to pick birch leaves with which to make mattresses for ourselves.

I remember that it was May 23rd, and very cold, but I was grateful to have something of reasonable comfort on which to rest at night.

We spent several days here at Wyschni-Woltschek, and my mattress became a cherished possession, second only to my precious rucksack which I still had been permitted to keep.

We were put to work during the day felling trees, cleaning them of limbs until they were long poles. Whether these were taken to sawmills, made into boards, used for posts or poles, I do not know. I do know that it was cold and I was weak, but almost in a miraculous way, God maintained my courage and my strength.

There were approximately a thousand prisoners of war in this camp, and we lived in primitive houses, built half-way out of the ground, with only a bit of the walls and the roof appearing above the level of the earth. But it was shelter, if damp and cold, and when a late snow fell, completely blanketing the ground, I was grateful that at least at night I could find a measure of rest.

It is strange how one's evaluations acclimate themselves to changing conditions. As you know, I stem from humble background, knowing little of the luxuries of life. But my wife had the touch of maternal genius in giving comfort to our menial home.

This was as far from that household comfort as despair is from hope. Yet I could be supremely grateful for a mattress on which to sleep.

Each night I thanked God for it, and each night — taking into consideration the dampness and the cold — I slept well.

12

At the very end of May, we made the long march on into Moscow. First across the countryside, then into suburban areas to a makeshift encampment. It seemed strange, being brought as prisoners to this great city, and I wondered if perchance we might be assigned to work detail. I wondered hopefully, harboring in my heart a gnawing fear at the thought of Siberia.

We soon learned the meaning of our visit. Our brief visit.

As had been predicted, we were to be exhibited to the Russian people as trophies of the conquest. Down broad boulevards, through residential avenues, across Red Square, we marched barefooted and in our frazzled uniforms behind large banners which, being in Russian, I could not translate.

Caesar did it, and so have other conqueror's whose footprints have fallen into type upon the pages of history. Even my blessed Lord was made to bear a Cross in ignomy before the cruel and curious eyes of the human mob. I suppose for us it was to be expected. The shame. The mental torment.

Wherever we went, civilians lined the thoroughfares, most of them ridiculing and mocking us, but some only staring as though we were a species of mankind they had thought never to see in the expanse of an entire lifetime. On some occasions, stones and even flower-pots were thrown at us, but for the most part the parades had a reasonable degree of orderliness to them.

Hatred inflamed the tongues of many of the men and beneath the din of marching, the cries of the crowd, I heard POW's scream profanely at their plight. Others, myself included, kept silent. Only marching. Marching, and hearing the crowds, until it became commonplace. For there was a certain anonymity to it all, if one could only face it that way.

Many of the prisoners were desperately ill, but had to keep on marching. I, too, wanted for strength, but thanked God that, in spite of the circumstances, He bestowed His sustaining hand so graciously upon me.

As you perhaps know, there exists a long, historic hatred between the Russian and the German people. The reasons for this are complex and I shall not go into them, sufficing it to say that the deepness of this feeling became quite evident as we made our exhibitory appearances.

"Nazi! Nazi!" some of them would cry, as we passed their way.

I wished, merely for the sake of human decency, that they could have known how far many of us were from any kind of obeisence to Nazi doctrine.

It was, I feel, this hatred of the Germans which caused the Russians to fight as valiantly as they did. Certainly it was not, at least in the fullest sense, loyalty to the Communist regime.

Few people realize the gigantic scope of wartime desertions which occurred among Soviet soldiers during the war, and the number of civilians who made their way out of Russia. It was, I am convinced, Hitler's invasion of Russia which brought the people together, stirring up a nationalism that reached the point of frenzy in contrast, for example, to the mediocre display of Russian military might against Finland a few years earlier. When one realizes that, of Russia's vast population, only five million actually are members of the Communist party, this becomes more understandable.

The fact, too, that the Russians realized they were fighting on the side of the United States played an important factor. Like the people of any country, they were at that time not too well informed of the actual policies of their government, little realizing that there existed even during the war those seeds of malice which would spawn open disagreement between the Soviet Union and the United States.

It is now common knowledge that when Hitler invaded Russia, Stalin and the men of the Kremlin had to make very careful plans, knowing full well that they had to compromise with the anti-Communist powers inside Russia and yet in no way weaken the Communist party.

Thus it was that, during the war, the program of the Communist party in the Soviet Union lay dormant. Nationalism became the issue. Russia was the great motherland and must be defended at all costs.

But while the program of the Communist Party lay dormant, it remained strong, even though large scale Red army defeats suffered early in the war left the Communist position shaky for quite some time.

What a strange weaving of fate it is that, in taking compromise measures so that they could bring into their fold not only anti-Communist groups inside Russia but also the good-will of the United States, the ultimate result was to so strengthen the hand of the Communists that they could press forward their quest for world domination at such a pace following the war as to completely over-ride any inconvenience which might have been imposed upon their program.

The wartime lull of organizational activity, in fact, heightened the movement's postwar successes. For, having gained prestige as an ally of freedom-loving nations, Russian Communists could the more successfully merchandise their post-war propaganda.

My purpose in telling you this is to give you something in the way of background as to the attitude of the Russian people toward us, their prisoners.

Forgive me once more for this repetition, but it was such a joy to me that I must make mention of the fact that, in all of this, there remained within my heart an unshakable love for these people. As I saw them lining the streets, remembering theirs was a government dedicated to the task of stamping out the memory of God from the face of the earth, my heart cried out in prayer.

I think I felt something of the emotion which must have

gone through the hearts of those who, remaining faithful, followed the Saviour on His way to Golgotha. Not that, in jeering us, these people were doing wrong, as did those who mocked my Lord, but rather the total situation, as I have mentioned, the fact that these people were in reality the prisoners and I the free man.

13

Our internment began in earnest now. Loaded again onto freight cars, we journeyed deep into Russian territory, north and ever east, into the mysterious, dreaded, terrible unknown that the world calls Siberia. I had searched my heart before, but I now probed even deeper into the facets of my Christian personality.

I will be honest with you. I trusted my Lord, but doubts came. They were jagged doubts, tearing mercilessly at my soul. Would a God, mindful of His children, submit one of them unto that which I was experiencing? Was it compatible to His greatness and wisdom that I should be subjected to the whims of a nation dedicated to destroying His glory from the face of the earth?

How good it was that I had the Bible in my rucksack. As we traveled, again by freight car, I read my Bible for hours at a time, grateful for the emission of enough daylight to make its pages legible. I would come to some portion, perhaps only a phrase, giving promise of His watchful care over His own and meditate for long periods of time. I remember particularly *My Grace is sufficient for thee*. It was like food and water and rest, like the song of freedom and the very presence of hope.

I was careful not to read my Bible in the presence of the Russian guards, lest they take it from me. I received persecution, nonetheless, in that many of those held captive with me scoffed at the very appearance of the Word of God.

"You must have the mind of an idiot," one man said to me. "What possible assistance can the platitudes of an outmoded book give to one who faces the bleak future ahead of you?"

"God never promises an easy way for those who trust Him," I replied. "He does, however, promise strength for every circumstance."

They laughed at this, the word spreading about throughout the boxcar, and men would come by where I was sitting to watch me reading the Book for want of anything else to arouse their curiosity.

Yes, many of them scoffed, but not all of them. There in that boxcar, moving ever onward to our final destination, I had the opportunity of bearing witness for Christ to a number of the prisoners. I cannot say that any of them confessed salvation at that time, but I did have the opportunity of thoroughly outlining God's marvelous pattern of redemption so clearly to several who, obviously moved by what they heard, were prepared to decide for Christ whenever they would simply open their hearts to Him.

Several more of our men died during that long journey. My heart ached for them, as I wanted to impart unto them the spiritual peace I had found, but there was rarely opportunity.

I did go over to the side of one man, desperately ill, and tried to open his soul to the grace of God. I shall never forget the look in his eyes. Too weak to speak, he looked up at me as though I were a madman. God's grace, it seemed, was the farthest thing for his mind in these surroundings. Even so, I knelt beside him and quietly quoted the Twenty-third Psalm.

"You can know this wonderful Lord as your Shepherd," I said. Then, as he closed his eyes—and I don't know whether he heard me or not, or, if hearing, could comprehend — I gave him verse after verse outlining God's wonderful plan of salvation.

14

We reached our camp by the second week of June.

As we stepped from our boxcar, out into the vastness of the Siberian countryside, intense melancholy came over me, a deep longing for my home.

Back in Germany, back where I lived, the flowers would be blooming and the air would be warm. But here, even in the month of June, snow lay on the ground like the torn fragments of a giant ghostly shroud.

I looked out at the great steppes of gray grass, gray because there was hardly summer enough for the green to materialize. I looked out at the vast forests, the mountains rising like silent sentinels on all sides. This was Siberia, known to many as the cemetery of brave souls. Here lay my future — for how long, I had not the slightest idea.

Ever since the day of the Czars, the Russians have used Siberia as a prison. Little wonder. It would be sheer suicide to try to escape. Except for the railroad tracks over which we were brought in, there was nothing but mountain and forest and wasteland. There were no roads. So far as I could ever tell, there was not even a trail leading to the outside world.

And even if one did attempt to escape, it would be death to go deeper into Siberia. There was no egress to the north. The south lay beyond human endurance. And to return west meant to come once more into Russia and sure apprehension.

Moscow does not deny the existence of what they call "Camps of Correctional Labor." When Vishinsky was Foreign Minister, he by a slip of the tongue actually referred to "Concentration Camps" in addressing the United Nations Assembly during October of 1947.

At the beginning, these slave labor camps in Siberia were intended to be means of terror and suppression. Stories of the awfulness of life in this vast wilderness would filter back to the Russian people, becoming a governmental wedge over any who would contemplate rebellion.

Today, Siberia still spells terror and suppression. But it has become, much more significantly, a strategic supply of manpower for the Russians. Whenever there comes a need for additional slaves, charges can be made against citizens of the country who are then sent out to Siberia to work in these camps. Foreign prisoners, such as ourselves, merely supplemented the throngs already there.

Deep concern for the welfare of my family tore again at my heart. If only our home had not been destroyed in the bombings, my anguish would have been less intense. If only I could be assured of my family's reasonable comfort, of the provision for food and shelter and clothing.

And then I was ashamed. Were there not many of these my comrades with similar anguish upon their hearts? Perhaps even greater? And did not many of them face these aftermath horrors of war without the indwelling sustenance of the Spirit of God?

Yes, I was ashamed as, anew, I committed my beloved wife and children into the Heavenly Father's care!

We were assigned to barrack-like buildings which, as I understand, had been built by previous prisoners of World War II. Due to the abundance of timber, these housing units, while rough, were adequate.

We were again given physical examinations and classified in work groups. I was placed in Work Group III, having been found in fair health, as compared to many others in our group, and would work eight hours per day. I would receive less food than those working in groups I and II, but they, on the other hand, worked ten, twelve and even fourteen hours per day.

The work was very hard. We cut down trees, trimming them of their branches for commercial use.

Each group was assigned a certain norm, which had to be accomplished during a specific time. If this norm, which was very high, was achieved, we were given an additional allotment of food. It was not often that we were able to reach the norm.

Our diet consisted almost entirely of *kapusta,* a sort of boiled, tasteless cabbage. We received it three time a day, at five o'clock in the morning, at noon, and again at five o'clock at night. Since we were working, we also received a half pound of bread.

To get a herring once a week was most fortunate. Herring, plus an additional 250 grams of bread, were awarded to those who exceeded the work norm. But, as I said, it was not often. *Kasch,* too, was available only when the norm had been fulfilled.

Day after day we worked in the timber. My strength ebbed with each setting of the sun. I became so weak, in fact, that I could not sleep well at nights. We had only thin mats, laid on the hard floor, and as I began losing weight, this became all the more uncomfortable.

At times, swinging an axe in the forest, I would black out almost completely. Once I did fall to the ground, but a Russian guard stood nearby and I quickly caught my senses and hurried to my feet pretending only to have stumbled. He looked at me strangely, then walked on.

While I continued to lose weight, my feet and knees began to swell, as dystrophy continued to manifest itself. I prayed earnestly to God for strength, for strength and for courage.

We were all vaccinated against smallpox but the equipment used was exceedingly poor and my inocculation gave me much pain. I was vaccinated on the arm, and some days I could barely swing an axe, so intense was the discomfort.

I had to watch myself more closely, as I began to suffer frequent attacks of melancholy and doubt. I would look sometimes to the horizon, toward the west, and wonder when if ever I would be reunited with my loved ones. The Lord gave me a wonderful wife, and I love her dearly. Our married life was one of harmony, not only toward each other but in our mutual faith. I missed her deeply, and sometimes, as I worked in the forest, I would imagine that I was back home, home with my beloved.

It was a very wonderful day when we were told that we could write to our nearest of kin. We were each given an official post card, used by prisoners of war, and told that we could write a maximum of twenty-five words. I think I must have pondered as do the poets, as I sent to my wife this communication:

Beloved,

I am well, safe, trusting. Thoughts of you daily. We shall meet again. Do not despair. My love to you always. Greet children. (Signed)

I gave my card to the nearest guard, as did others about me, and my heart breathed gratitude to God for this opportunity of informing my wife that I was alive. In all the confusion of the last days of war, I could not hope that anything in the way of an official message had gotten to her.

I despaired momentarily, however, when — only a few moments after turning in my card — a German-speaking officer came to me.

He held the card in his hand and, looking at me rather menacingly, said, "You have sent a code message!"

I looked up at him, not understanding.

He turned the card toward me, and pointed at what I had written. "This!"

"I will rewrite it, if you wish," I said. "It is not in code. If it seems so, it is because I wanted to say as much as I could in the amount of words allotted to us."

I trembled, for no one spoke so boldly.

He glared at me a moment, and then turned and walked away, and it was to be many, many long weeks before I learned whether or not my message had reached its destination.

"Did you send a code message?" one of the prisoners asked me. Anger rose in his eyes. "Have you no sense, man? Don't you know that if one of us is disobedient, all will suffer?"

"I sent no code," I said.

"Of course he didn't," another man said. "They are merely trying to intimidate us. They want us to be on guard at all times, lest any one should try to send out information."

Still another of the prisoners spoke. "What difference would it make?" he laughed, a dry, acid laugh. "Are they afraid the *Wehrmacht* will rise up again, and come to liberate us?"

While we were under almost constant surveillance, we did have a measure of freedom at night, after we had been locked in our barracks. We would gather and sing some of the old familiar songs of Germany. I tried to get the men to sing hymns, and they did occasionally.

But their favorite song was *"Heimat, Deinne Sterne,"* which means, "Home, The Stars Shine Over Your Sky." This had been a very popular pre-war song in Germany, and it stirred up great emotion among us. So much so, in fact, that one night as we sang, a young prisoner lost complete control of himself. Rushing madly about the barracks, he screamed, "My fiance! We were to get married as soon as I returned from the war! My fiance! She doesn't know if I am alive or dead! She will marry someone else! She will marry someone else!"

Several of the men subdued him, holding him down to the floor. He continued screaming, and they held their hands over his mouth.

The door unlocked, and a Russian guard entered.

"What *is* it?" he asked. One of our men, who had become an unofficial spokesman for us, stepped forward. "It is only a boy," he said. "He is lonesome for home."

Then, turning, he pointed to the boy, still being subdued to the floor.

"Let him stand!" the guard commanded.

The men released their grip. The lad stood to his feet, his face wild with fright and tension.

"Come!" the guard commanded, motioning to the boy.

The lad looked about him, as though hoping that someone would stand to his defense. No one spoke. No one dared. Slowly, he made his way over to the officer.

Together, they disappeared through the door out into the darkness and we never saw the boy again. During the night, one of the men in our barracks insisted he heard the crack of rifle fire. I do not know. I heard nothing, though I lay awake far into the night, my heart sick for such a young life to be subjected to the awfulness of this fate.

15

As time went on, the attitude of the Russians toward us stiffened. We were brought in for lectures, told that the war was over and that Russia had taken a place of leadership among all the nations of earth.

"You are being prepared, even during this temporary incarceration," one officer told us, "to return to a world that will belong to the people. Your cooperation, your attention to the privileges extended, will hasten that day."

We did not know for sure what he meant, and the short speech was much discussed that evening in our barracks.

"Do you think the war is really over?" one man asked me.

"I wouldn't know," I said. "Surely it must be, judging from the almost total collapse we saw on the eastern front."

"I would give a week's rations for a newspaper," the man said. And I think I agreed with him.

There were many check-ups and examinations. Usually they came unexpectedly, in the middle of the night. The door to the barracks would fling open and bright spotlights be flashed across the sleepers on the floor.

These examination periods were called *filzen,* with each prisoner required to lay out his valuables upon his cot, strip off all his clothes, and stand at attention.

Of course, the very first time this happened, many of our cherished valuables were confiscated. I watched in terror as my Bible was examined with the greatest of care, apparently in the search for secret messages.

I am sure the Russians had never seen a Bible before, for they gathered about it like children looking at some new curiosity and muttered back and forth to each other.

I longed to open my mouth and proclaim Christ to those men.

One of the officers did say, in reasonable understandable German, "Is not he the one who tried to send a code message by mail?"

I trembled with fear.

This evoked considerable amount of additional chattering between the officers, as they stood examining my Bible. Deep, deep in my heart, I pleaded with God not to permit the precious Book to be confiscated. Yet, even as I prayed, I thanked God for the fact that I had been able to lay so much of it by memory into my heart. Standing there, the words of the Psalmist gave assurance to me, *Thy Word have I hid in my heart.* That they could never take!

After a lengthy examination of my Bible, the maps in the back were torn out, and the book was handed back to me. I almost cried I was so grateful.

The very next day, I was again asked to produce my Bible for examination. But it still was not confiscated.

This attention given to the Bible on the part of the Russians stirred up mingled reactions among the prisoners. A

57

few of them wondered if perhaps there might be something in the way of religious interest stirred up, which would ameliorate our lot in the camp. Others, however, became angry, and even insisted that I destroy the Bible.

"These men are atheists," one prisoner said. "You will bring reprisals upon all of us, keeping a Bible in your possession."

I do not know what the result of this statement might have been since a number of the men agreed, had it not been that another prisoner spoke up. "Suppose he destroys the Bible, and then is asked to produce it again?"

"What difference would that make?" someone asked.

"The answer is obvious," came the reply. "The Russians will think then that the Book does have some significance so far as our security as prisoners is concerned. No, now that the Bible has been seen, the man should keep it."

A brief mumbling followed. One of the men, who had stepped forward as though to demand the Book from me, glared silently at me for a moment, then turned.

I could not restrain the tears which came to my eyes, tears of gratitude to God for prohibiting these men from taking His Word from me.

The fact that the Russians had taken this interest in the Bible proved a real boon to me in my witnessing, and I had an opportunity to speak to many whom otherwise I might never have reached with the Gospel message.

The most difficult part of witnessing was that the men so often wanted God to give them physical deliverance, as if receiving Christ as Saviour would mean that they would suddenly be released from the Russian prison camp. I tried to explain that God's children through the ages have been subjected to the same testings as have befallen those outside of Christ, and that God does not promise physical blessing in all instances. I tried to show them — I tried desperately — that being a child of God means even more in time of discomfort than when all is well.

I am sorry to say, in too many instances, the realization

that I could not promise any great physical gain caused inquirers to turn way.

Not all, however. During even those early days, I had the joy of seeing two men confess faith in Christ. One of them, very quiet, gave only faint indication in the weeks to come of any transformation in his heart. But the other, all praise to God, clearly indicated that he had become a new creature in Christ.

16

By July, the snow had at last gone, and it became dry and hot — hot at least for those of us who continued laboring in the forests. There were some of the men who rebelled against the guards and were punished, but for the most part everyone took upon himself an attitude of resignation and life became so routine as to be humdrum.

Some of the men did organize an orchestra, using instruments fashioned by hand. It was a crude attempt, at best, but it gave us many evenings of enjoyment, and the men became quite adept at playing some of the old songs of Germany.

Several of the men fashioned needles from wood and, using string as thread and old discarded pieces of cloth received from the officials, did crude knitting and needlepoint.

Other than appearing for work, I did little in the way of physical activity. My strength continued to ebb, as my feet and knees swelled from the presence of dystrophy, and I became so weary and ill at times I could not read my Bible.

Many nights, unable to sleep, I lay staring at the blackness, as intense seizures of depression came over me. I recognized these as attacks of Satan, taking advantage of my weakness, and although my mind would be numb with weariness and pain, I would quote Scripture verse after Scripture verse, mingling with the Word of God the cry of my own heart that the Lord would keep me faithful to Himself.

Working became a terrifying experience, and although I tried to do my share each day, sometimes it was almost impossible to raise an axe above my head. One guard, realizing my plight, showed me kindness, and assigned me to a crew that cleared away brush after it had been trimmed from tree trunks. But this was little better.

One morning, just as we were about to leave for work, I received a summons to appear before the medical committee. Apparently my name had been turned in by the guards as one physically unfit to work in the forests and the thought of what the consequences of this might mean struck terror to my heart.

By now, my legs had become so swollen that I could only walk with the most extreme difficulty. So it took the doctors only a few moments to diagnose my condition.

"You will go to the hospital," I was told. "It is north, about twenty kilometers."

"How will I go?" I asked.

"Walk," was the answer. Obviously, there was no thought of my attempting escape in my physical condition.

The head of the committee penned my name and his own signature to a certificate, and handed it to me. "You will give this to the official at the admissions office of the hospital camp," he said.

I took the certificate, paused just a moment, then turned and went outside. It was strange, being in the barracks area this time of day. All of the other men had gone out with the work crews. I felt strangely alone. Off in the distance, I heard the sound of toil, but otherwise all was quiet.

I stepped out into a clearing, and turned my eyes northward. Twenty kilometers! Nearly ten miles! I could never possibly walk so far in my condition!

In the weeks that I had been at this camp, I had never left the premises other than to proceed into the nearby forest for work. Even so short a trip as twenty kilometers to the north was like going on a long journey. I wondered what would happen if I did not go. Or if I should attempt and fall, overcome with pain and weariness, at the roadside.

Kind Heavenly Father, I prayed, *I am completely dependent upon Thy guidance. Please help me!*

It was like a miracle. A horse-drawn carriage, which daily brought food to our camp, stopped nearby. The driver was a German prisoner.

"Why are you not out with the work crew?" he asked, looking cautiously about.

I stumbled over to the carriage. "I am to go to the hospital," I replied.

"The hospital camp is twenty kilometers to the north," he said.

"I know, but I cannot possibly walk so far." I showed him my swollen ankles.

"I am going," he said. "I go each day. You may ride with me."

A great well-spring of gratitude to God lifted from my soul, as I got into the carriage and we made our way out onto the road toward the hospital camp. A sparrow flew overhead, darting back and forth for a moment before disappearing toward the forest. And I remembered the Saviour's promise that not one of them could fall to the earth without His permission. Nor need I, one of His children, ever pass beyond His watchful eye.

17

I found the hospital much like the camp from which I had come, a hospital only in the sense that it was kept clean and that limited facilities had been provided for medical treatment. The barracks had been painted a dull white. A man on crutches hobbled into view, followed shortly by one POW pushing another in a makeshift wheel chair; a Russian medical insignia adorned the unguarded gate, all attesting to the fact this was a place of the healing arts.

"You will get off here," the man who drove the carriage said, as we drew to a halt before a small hut which appeared to be the admissions building. "Best of everything."

I climbed slowly from my perch, carefully testing my legs as they touched the ground. Then, looking up, I said, "Thank you. I am very grateful. You came to me in my need by the hand of God."

He laughed. "You're sure God didn't lose His bearings in this wilderness long ago?"

"I'm quite sure," I asserted.

"Giddap," he called to his team.

The conveyance moved on and, hesitating a moment, I walked up to the admissions building. Here, again, I hesitated, not knowing whether to knock on the door or wait for someone to come—or enter. I decided to enter.

A fellow German prisoner, who had lost an arm during the war, sat at a table just inside the door going through some cards which he had taken out of a small file. He looked up abruptly as I entered.

"Why are you here?" he asked brusquely. "This is the admissions building."

"I know," I said, taken aback somewhat by his attitude.

"Then why are you here?" he asked.

"I have come for admission," I said.

"Where are the others?"

"There are no others."

"You mean you came alone?"

I nodded, not sure whether or not I should disclose the fact that I had been fortunate in getting a ride.

"You walked?" he asked.

I handed him the medical dismissal slip I had received from the other camp, and he took it without comment, except to mumble "dystrophy" and glance momentarily at me.

He took out a file card and asked several questions as to my identity, when and where I had been captured, my estimated weight, height, medical history.

Then he stood and motioned for me to follow him.

We went outside and he led the way to another building about half a city block distant. Here we met a German prisoner who supplied me with bedding, eating utensils and a worn but clean hospital garment.

A short distance beyond this building stood the barracks to which I had been assigned. Immediately upon entering, my heart lifted its voice in praise to God. There were cots with thin but sturdy mat-like mattresses — sheer luxury by comparison to sleeping on the floor as had been the case at the last camp.

I was surprised not to find any patients in the ward, this being a hospital barracks, but said nothing at the moment.

We walked to an empty cot and my guide said, "This will be yours." He handed me a card. "Fill out your name and address and the details requested. Place this in the bracket provided at the foot of the bed."

He turned to leave.

"Shall I stay here alone?" I asked.

He smiled briefly. "I should have told you," he said. "This ward is for those who are not seriously ill. Everyone in this ward works and so shall you. The patients are on assignments. They will return prior to time for the evening meal."

He left.

It was now about the hour of noon, and I had no food nor was there the promise of any, but I did not mind. Hunger had become so common with me that it passed at times unnoticed.

I needed rest more than food and quickly made my cot and lay down. "O God!" I remember praying aloud. "I thank Thee for this provision for my bodily need!"

Desperately tired, I fell sound asleep, more soundly than I can remember ever having slept since my incarceration. When I awakened, it was to the sound of many voices and the bustle

63

of activity within the barracks. I lifted to my elbow and, trying to shake sleep from my eyes, peered out at the maelstrom of activity about me.

The man who occupied the cot to my right came over and sat down, saying, "You are new here, Comrade. Did you just arrive today?"

"Yes I did," I said, telling him my name to introduce myself.

He told me his name, and extended his hand.

"We have all been out on our work detail," he said. "It will soon be time to eat. You will come with us? Don't worry if you have no specific instructions. They are loosely organized here."

"What is it like here?" I asked.

"About like any other prisoner-of-war camp," he said, "unless one is so ill that he requires special hospitalization. The food is better, considerably better, and you'll probably gain some weight. The work is tolerable. We have been clearing brush to establish a firebreak in the forest. A German supervises us, and we only work as hard as we wish."

A bugle sounded off in the distance, and the man said, "That is mess call. We had better hurry."

Already, the others had begun filing out the door, and I stood and joined the line. Once outside, we marched a considerable distance to the mess hall. Inside, single file, we passed serving tables, and then went over to small benches, with no tables, to eat.

It was as though I had been here as long as the longest man, for no one paid any attention to me, no one asked any questions or offered instructions. Why had I not been contacted by anyone other than the German prisoner at the admissions building? What would happen to me henceforth? Would I receive no work assignment? Would I become lost in the mass of humanity here, like some stray animal who has wandered long and far and identified himself with new surroundings?

I continued to wonder when, having eaten, we made our

way back to the barracks once more. I stretched out on my bed and I lay thinking for a considerable length of time. I wanted to read my Bible, but thought it best to wait until I had become more acclimated to the surroundings. Instead, I recited from memory many portions of the Bible and offered prayers of thanks to God and new requests for guidance in this place where He had permitted me to find myself.

There was no light in the barracks, as had been true in the previous camp, and with the setting of the sun came darkness. I found this restful, so did not mind.

"How long have you been a prisoner-of-war?" the man next to me asked, and I told him. "You are fortunate," he said. "I was captured during the first month of the Stalingrad campaign."

"You have been in Siberia all this time?" I asked, shuddering at the thought.

"No," he replied. "I was assigned to a work detachment just outside Moscow." He remained quiet for a moment. Then he said, "I like this much better. At least one is not subject to the prying eyes of onlookers."

"I know what you mean," I told him, relating my own experiences during the march down the streets of Moscow.

"Well, it's whatever is in the stars for us, I guess," he said, taking a deep breath as if in resignation.

"It is whatever God wills," I said softly.

He lifted himself up, and in the remnant light that filtered through the narrow window above our heads, I caught the focus of his eyes intent upon me. "You will find Siberia's coldest reception of all to those who are religious," he said. "God never sets foot inside Siberia, Comrade."

"I sense Him very near," I said.

He looked at me another moment. "You speak as though you mean it," he said. "And you have been even this long a prisoner?"

"Every day," I said, "my faith in God becomes more meaningful to me."

"It will change," he said. "It will change."

Then he settled down upon his cot and did not speak. I turned on my side and remained in a period of meditation and prayer for an hour or more until, once again, I fell asleep.

18

We were awakened an hour before dawn, by searchlights beamed across the barracks and by vocal command. *"Paschly!"* a voice snapped. *"Paschly!"*

Quickly, everyone arose and began getting dressed. A Russian guard placed near the door a dimly lit oil lantern which cast sufficient light for each one to find his clothing and tidy his bed. Then once more, at the signal of a bugle, we marched to the mess hall for a breakfast of gruel which I found surprisingly palatable.

Any thought I may have had of being lost in the crowd vanished immediately after breakfast when an officer called for attention to give the day's assignments. He called my name and said for me to stand on my feet which, of course, I did. In understandable German, he told me that I had been assigned to the bakery. Then he called the name of another man who stood, and instructed me that I was to report to him for details.

Immediately after dismissal, I sought out this man and we walked together to the bakery.

"You are fortunate," he said, looking me over momentarily. "You have not had sufficient food, but you will get all you want to eat, at least while you are working in my detail."

The ovens and bakery implements were of the crudest design, almost to the point of amusement — a factor so often apparent in all my observations of the Russians. They appeared abnormally backward in many of the menial pursuits of life, as though they had relegated certain needed advancements to insignificance the better to shoulder those responsibilities which would more quickly bring to realization their primal ambitions.

"You are hungry?" the German in charge asked.

"I haven't known a full stomach since I left the Fatherland," I told him.

"If you can tolerate bread, we can change that," he said.

He then motioned for me to follow him into a side room. "There," he said, pointing to a large stack of loaves ready for delivery to the mess hall. "Eat."

I looked at the bread and at him. *Maybe the man is a sadist,* I thought, *and he wants to get me into trouble.*

"Eat, Comrade!"

"I do not want to disobey the rules," I said cautiously.

He stroked his fat stomach. "Rules?" he chortled. "I make the rules here, and I say eat!"

"But I do not need to take good loaves. Are there no crumbs?"

He looked at me a moment. "You are an honest man, aren't you? I hope they leave you always in the bakery. Come."

I followed him to another room. There, in a large basket, lay a bountiful supply of imperfect loaves.

"I keep these out and smuggle them to my friends," he said. "A man has to have some pride. I want the loaves I send to the kitchen to be only the perfectly shaped specimens of my art. Now, Comrade, eat!"

And I ate. Like a madman almost. One loaf. Two. From time to time the baker left, but he would come back to watch me. Only when I protested that I could not consume another bite did he assign me a simple chore with which to begin my tenure as his assistant.

During my first eight days at the camp, I worked in the bakery, eating every crumb, every morsel, I could lay my hands upon. I especially enjoyed the assignment of getting yeast, as I found it rather good tasting. There would always be two of us, carrying a container on a stick, and it was only natural that as we loaded our container, some would splash over the side. This we would consume for ourselves to the last minute particle.

During my second day at camp, I was taken from my work detail and brought to a special medical center for examination. I received a rather thorough examination from a Russian doctor. He asked me no questions — probably he could not speak a word of German — but went over my body from my head to my feet. He sounded my chest, took numerous specimens, spent a considerable amount of time going over my back with his stethoscope. All the time, he made profuse notes on a medical report sheet.

He was completely impassive, perhaps bored, as though I were a mere machine he was trying to tune into working condition for the needs of his country. I especially watched as he made the notations, and wondered what they might say — all manner of imaginations going through my mind. Suppose he listed me as machinery beyond repair and not suitable for further use?

I trembled, and I prayed.

After the examination, I returned once more to my work. It was a rather disconcerting experience in that no prediction had been made as to what my tenure would be at the hospital. However, later that afternoon, upon returning to the barracks, I was given a bottle of medication to be taken in the morning and in the evening. I presumed the medication was to combat the effects dystrophy had made upon my body.

"How have you and God fared today?" the man next to me asked, as I sat down upon my cot.

I looked at him, saw that he was smiling, so I smiled back and said, "Very well. How have you and God fared?"

"I didn't run across Him all day," the man said, breaking now into a dull laugh.

"Well, I'm sorry to hear that," I said, "For I'm sure you were mistaken in thinking that He is not here."

"In atheistic Russia?" he asked, furrowing his forehead.

I opened my rucksack and took out my Bible. I shall never forget the alarm that registered upon his face.

"Surely you will admit that God is existant wherever one finds His Word?" I said.

"Put that back!" he exclaimed, looking nervously about. "Surely you have not brought that into view in the presence of a Russian guard."

"Not here," I said, "for I have just come. But the guards have known elsewhere that I have my Bible with me."

"Put it away, I tell you! Don't be a fool!"

I did not want to irritate him, but neither did I wish to compromise my witnessing. Stretching out upon my cot, I opened the blessed Book and began reading. From the periphery of my vision, I saw him turn to the opposite side of his cot, as though to insure against any possibility of his being identified with my action.

I had not read long until a Russian guard came to the door, commanding all of us to follow him. I put my Bible back into my rucksack, noticing as I did the scrutiny with which my barrack's mate watched me, and then stood to my feet.

We marched to a building a short distance away, large enough to seat all of the ambulatory prisoners at the camp. It was plain to see that this was something in the way of a classroom, or at least a lecture hall, for there was a large blackboard at the front and a lecturn.

A Russian officer came in, stepped up to the lectern and began speaking.

With neither excitement nor rancor, the speaker outlined the history of the Communist movement. Omitting any political references, he pointed up communism as a means to happiness, as a solution to the problems which beset the world such as overpopulation, unfair distribution of wealth, improper evaluation of the rights of the individual.

Obviously, this was not the first of his lectures, but one in a series being given to the men at the camp. Yet the simplicity with which he presented the material, going back to outline that which had been previously covered, made it remarkably easy to follow his continuity.

His voice had a pleading quality to it, giving evidence of the man either having an adeptness at sincerity or fully believing in what he said.

And, to be sure, there was nothing to be criticized in what he did say. Except, of course, that I could not agree with his insistence upon the communist way of life being the solution to the problems of the world.

I looked about me at the faces of many of the other men. Some sat in quiet resignation, some appeared bored, others showed resentment, but many eagerly received the words being spoken to them. Upon the faces of the latter ones, I witnessed for the first time the magic spell that the Communist message can cast upon the human heart.

How I wished I could have stepped to the front and, my Bible in hand, proclaimed from the Word of God the true solution to the problems besetting humanity! For the Gospel grips the heart as nothing else can, including the promised panacea of communism, if only there were as many zealous hearts propagating its message as there are expounding the tenets of Marxian philosophy!

19

I remained at the hospital camp for about a month, during which time my initial examination by a physician and the one I received on the day of my discharge constituted the only specific medical attention given me. There were no checks as to temperature, blood count, or pressure. Not even so much as the rate of my pulse. While I did take daily doses of the medicine initially prescribed for me, I question seriously whether it had any appreciable effect upon my physical condition. The improved housing conditions, and the additional supply of food, however, did help me considerably, and so when I received my second examination, it was followed by the decree that I should be transferred once more to a work camp.

What examination I did receive was highly impersonal. As though I were an animal retired from hitch for awhile until a hoof healed. For I began to sense that I was not so much a prisoner-of-war as, rather, a statistic on "loan" from Germany for the purpose of expediting the reconstruction of Russia.

I presume the Soviet government felt justified in exacting our servitude — considering it right to obtain tangible recourse for the material losses inflicted by the German *Wehrmacht* and *Luftwaffe*.

Together with some twenty others, I joined a contingent which set off on foot down a narrow roadway leading from the hospitalization area, a lurking fear of the unknown once more storming the walls of faith which bastioned my heart.

In the armed services of his own country, a soldier receives little information as to where he is to be transferred in the course of duty. Much less did we know the day-to-day fate that awaited us. I wondered if perhaps each man's destiny had been carefully plotted, beginning with a lesser degree of banishment and then progressing on into more advanced stages until "man's inhumanity to man" would plunge to the ultimate.

I wondered and trembled.

We did not march far that day, only about three hours distance, but a feeling of insecurity came over me such as I had not experienced in all the qualms of my earlier experiences as a prisoner-of-war.

I have never learned what is the geographical pattern of the Siberian detention areas — though I subsequently learned we were near the Arctic Ocean — but I would presume they were located in clusters. For once I had entered Siberia itself, I was never transferred a great distance away. Yet, even so, each move gave me the feeling of being transported farther and farther from my loved ones, farther and farther from freedom, farther and farther from any hope of a compatible tomorrow upon earth. It was like one of those dreams which come just at the brink of consciousness, when one is near enough to awakening to realize that, however horrible the dream may be, it is indeed only a dream and shall soon pass. But in all my lifetime, I had never known a dream to extend so long, and as the days passed, I realized that this was reality, totally unreal though it might be.

I could understand how even the unknown drives men from their senses, apart from any physical or mental punitive aspects of imprisonment. Where would tomorrow be spent and how? When would release come, be it by death or liberation? These questions could gnaw at a man's mind until the root and sap of rationality were gone.

I thanked God for the sustaining ballast of my faith in Him! Never once did there come a time when I looked into the abyss of uncertainty, seeing only darkness hiding the true content of the bottom of that abyss, without finding that, in turning to God, my heart came at peace. The Lord gave me confidence that, however far I might be from my loved ones and, indeed, from those who gave allegiance to the Saviour of Calvary, I never once escaped the watchful care of my God.

I believe that I speak these words by divine directive, my friends, for this is a world which, because of it's utter depravity, cannot tolerate the demands of a Holy God upon the human heart. Thus it becomes altogether possible — if not, in such a world as this, probable — for many of God's children to be called upon to bear witness of their faith in Him at the expense of great phyiscal suffering. Should this befall you, take heart! God is never so near as at that moment when one has come to the farthest point from physical happiness and, realizing the span of lifetime is but the passing of a moment in God's sight, the believer lifts the eye of his heart heavenward and sees the endless vistas of eternity laden with the bountiful pleasures for which the human soul was intended. Suffering, however it comes, is a refiner's fire and, with Job, the believer can say: *"When He hath tried me, I shall come forth as gold.*

The camp to which I was transferred was pronounced "Seelager." I never saw the correct spelling. It lay deep in the woods, along the bank of a beautiful river. Apparently it had been used for a long time, because the buildings were old and gave evidence of the installation having been given extended use.

Tree trunks came floating down the river, obviously from some other work camp above us, and we had to get the logs out onto the bank and into freight cars.

It was intense work, much too demanding for my ebbing physical strength, although we did receive somewhere near normal food allotments, half a pound of bread and a half pint of *kash* daily.

Inadequate sleep gave me my greatest difficulty, even more so than the hard work. First of all, at first, I had no mattress and had to sleep upon the hard floor. When I asked for one, the German POW in charge of my work detail said, "You'll have to wait until someone is transferred or otherwise removed from the barracks. When you see this happen, grab for his mattress. No one will supply it for you. But don't steal one. A man can get his throat slit for that."

Not only did I have to sleep on the hard board floor, but because of the intensely heavy work, the men came to the barracks each night totally exhausted, with the result that snoring reached outlandish proportions. I would lie awake sometimes feeling as though I were in some kind of woodworking plant, with saws active in all directions.

During my days in the German army I had gone nights with little if any sleep, but then I had had more physical strength with which to combat the deprivation of rest. Now, my strength all but gone, I wondered if I could possibly live.

Then one day, while at work retrieving logs from the river, I suffered an injury to my left thumb. At first, I thought it had been horribly crushed, but examination by the camp medic — I do not think he was actually a doctor — seemed to indicate that only the flesh had been badly mangled.

I was given an easier assignment, requiring only the use of my good hand, and I hoped that within a few days the thumb would heal, for it gave me much discomfort. Instead, however, infection set in.

I thought surely they would return me to the hospital, especially when the infection became so acute that my entire hand became swollen beyond its normal size. But they didn't.

The Word of God became like bread to me, giving not only encouragement to my soul but motivation to my being. I would read for hours, becoming oblivious to my misery, the state of my existence, the very world itself.

It was during one such reading that a fellow prisoner came to me and, tapping my arm, said, "You are asking for trouble, Comrade." I looked up at him. "Reading a Bible here," he continued. "You are a prisoner of the Communists, my friend."

"I have had my Bible with me constantly," I said, "and—"

"What good is it to you?" he broke in. And before I could offer a reply, he continued, "I have been a prisoner for two years. Have you gone through a Siberian winter? This is paradise compared to the cold hell of January and February! God can do you little good when the frost bites the marrow of your bones! I have learned a secret, Comrade, and I pass it on to you. You would be wise to find its worth as I have. Think of yourself as no more than an animal, for that is what you are. A dog, a horse, whatever you choose. So you live, so you work, so you eat, or so you starve and die. What difference does it make?"

"It makes the difference of all eternity!" I exclaimed.

"Do not speak so loud!" he cautioned. "The Russians have no assignment for preachers! They assign grave-digging details for men like you!"

"You do not understand," I said. "You do not realize that—"

"I understand!" he interrupted. "Perhaps I should say I once understood. My home is Wiesbaden. I was a communicant in the church there. I read the Bible. I listened to the preaching. I put no stock in the ways of the Nazis. I was a man of faith, one who believed in God. And do not say that I had only a head religion, for I have heard that argument. I loved God in my heart. I thought I knew the meaning of love and hope."

He stood there, like a living corpse, and I wanted to speak to him but could not.

"I have been here two years, Comrade. During that time I have had three communications from Wiesbaden. One from my mother, telling of her love and prayers. One from my sister, telling of my mother's death. And one from my brother, telling me that my wife had filed a petition for divorce so that she could marry again." He turned to me and his lips curled. "Do you think a man can believe in that kind of world? Oh, you speak of faith in God now, but you wait. Faith can no more survive the cold of Siberia than a living being could survive the heat of an Essen blast furnace."

"I insist you do not understand," I said. "Faith is eternal. Faith cannot die, whatever peril may befall the human frame."

"Faith cannot die?" he asked, sneering, "You say that only because you have never seen it die. But you shall see. You shall see faith die in the rot of your own pessimism. You shall see hope die. You shall see yourself die, Comrade, even though you continue to serve as a human mechanism for the use of the Russians. Yes, you shall see."

"But this is only the present," I protested. "Life at its longest is but a moment in comparison to the expanse of eternity. I do not question that you have suffered, or that I shall suffer. The Apostle Paul says in Romans: *For I reckon that the sufferings of this present time are not worthy to be compared with the glory which shall be revealed in us.* And in Corinthians, we read: *For our light affliction, which is but for a moment, worketh for us a far more exceeding and eternal weight of glory; While we look not at the things which are seen, but at the things which are not seen: for the things which are seen are temporal; but the things which are not seen are eternal.* Do not lose hope, my friend!"

"Lose hope?" he asked. "I have none to lose. It is all gone — gone forever — as shall also any hope that yet remains within your own heart."

I tried to counsel with him from the Scriptures, but it was of no use.

"You could as well talk to the trunk of one of the trees outside," he said. "You do not now understand, but you shall." He turned and walked away, muttering, "You shall, Comrade."

A great wave of fear swept over me, as I lay thinking. Could it be that this man had known the same faith I now knew, that he once trusted in God as I now trusted? And, if so, could it be that faith and hope would one day die in my own heart? Or had he been numbered with that multitude whom the Word of God describes as *having a form of godliness but denying the power thereof?*

O God! I prayed. *Show me anew the reality of Thyself!*

And, desperately, I turned once more to the Word of God and spent the next several hours reading every portion on faith and hope and confidence I could find, as well as passages denoting the greatness of our Heavenly Father.

20

My infected thumb grew no better and I went several times to the medic attached to our unit. He would only dress it, give me aspirin to alleviate the pain and tell me to return in a day or so.

My entire hand continued swelling, and dagger-like thrusts

of pain travelled all the way up my arm to my shoulder. I dreaded the thought of acute blood poisoning here with virtually nothing in the way of medical care.

Then one night, we were suddenly ordered from our barracks and led on a long foot march to a camp deeper in the woods. Everyone was put to work felling and trimming trees, our entire unit being given a daily norm all but impossible to reach.

Summer had gone. It was September. The chill warning of winter pressed upon us from the north.

I remember how I stood in a secluded area of brush, looking at my hand. Could it be that my God, realizing the winter would be unbearable, had sent this infection to my hand so that death would mercifully relieve me of even greater suffering?

At that moment, an insatiable desire to live came upon me — a feeling of destiny, the conviction deep in my soul that God had a ministry for me here in the Siberian forests. Perhaps it may seem naive to you, but I grasped my aching hand and lifted it heavenward, pleading with God to restore it to normalcy again.

Swinging an ax during the long hours of the day, each thrust against timber causing my hand to ache as though it, not the wood, had felt the cutting blow, I blacked out entirely on several occasions. Yet I did not fall to the ground. Miraculously, I remained standing and would sometimes come out of a semi-trance to find myself swinging the ax as though nothing had happened.

Surely it was the sustaining hand of God!

There was nothing in the way of a medic at this camp, not even fresh bandage with which to keep my wound clean. Water throughout this area of Siberia was exceedingly rare, distributed literally by ounces, and I could not so much as soak my thumb in the hope of drawing out some of the poison resident there.

On September 11th, something happened which may seem

commonplace to you, but which evoked silent paeans of praise from the depth of my heart.

We were served potatoes.

Commonplace to you? Perhaps. There was a day when I partook of potatoes with no more than a nominal grace at the table in thanks to God. But these were the first potatoes I had had since my imprisonment, and while they were served completely plain, they were to me like the rarest of delicacies!

The potatoes seemed to give me new strength, and with the strength, renewed encouragement. Work stepped up in all phases of our assignment, and the Russians kept potatoes on the menu.

It was for only a short time, however. Four days to be specific. On September 15th, we were transferred to what I learned was the main camp of that entire area, a place called Sauna.

By comparison with the previous camps, Sauna was quite modern. There was sufficient water for us to bathe. All of us had grown extensive beards, which were now shaved. Our heads were shaved, too, as a sanitary measure.

The infection on my thumb had now reached an alarming stage but, praise be to God, there was a German Army doctor at Sauna.

"This is not good!" he exclaimed, the moment he had laid bare my ailing digit. "How long has this been?"

I told him.

"There is little mercy in the world!" he gasped. "It is a wonder you have lived!"

"It is the grace of God," I said. I could not withhold the comment.

"Do you think so?" he asked, not looking up from his task of cleaning the wound. "Perhaps you are right."

"I'm sure of it," I said.

He looked up at me. "So you are, I thought it was only a passing comment."

I smiled, not knowing quite what to say.

78

"Well," he said, also smiling, "it is good you can keep your faith in God. It is good." Then he went back to caring for my thumb, adding, "With proper medication . . . and the grace of God, as you say . . . I think we can nurse this horrid spectacle back to normal. I shall prescribe five days of complete rest for you, and you might pray, too, that the officials will think kindly of my suggestion. You ought not to use this for at least five days."

21

The authorities abided by the recommendation of the German doctor, and for five days I did not work. It was wonderful how my injured thumb responded to medication and rest.

But God had an even greater blessing for me. There was a shoe repair shop at the camp, which I happened to pass one day. Glancing inside, I saw to my amazement a dear brother in Christ whom I had known from civilian life!

I ran to him, calling out his last name, and as he turned to me, a look of complete incredulity spread across his face. We stood for a moment, facing each other. Then he spoke my name and rushed to me and embraced me.

I began to laugh, the first time I had laughed since I had been taken prisoner. This dear man was a twin, and while I had known him and his brother well, I could not for the life of me determine which of the two he was.

I asked him and he laughed as heartily as did I in telling me his name.

He had to return to his work, but I slipped cautiously over beside him, keeping an eye on his supervisor who seemed not to mind. After a few hesitant moments, we engaged in hearty conversation. We spoke of our fellowship in the old days, of his loved ones and of mine, of our days in the army and our capture and what had happened to us since we became prisoners-of-war. It was wonderful therapy to hearts knotted by uncertainty.

But most of all, we spoke of our kindred faith in the Lord Jesus Christ!

Except for those whom I had been privileged to lead to the Saviour, this was the first Christian brother with whom I had had fellowship. It was, in actuality, the first real fellowship — since he had walked with the Lord many years and had a heart full of the treasures of the Word of God.

He did not have a Bible, his having been confiscated at the time of his capture and when, at the earliest opportunity, I brought him mine, he grasped it from me and held it to his bosom and wept like a child. Then, opening the blessed Book, he turned from page to page, reading a verse here, a phrase there.

"The Word of God!" he exclaimed. "The Word of God!"

I, too, wept.

"I have been grateful for those scriptures which, since my conversion, had been laid store in my heart," he told me. "It sustained me all this time. But this is the entire Word of God, every morsel of it; The blessed Book! The Blessed Book!"

"We can share it," I said to him. "I will leave it with you for several days, since you have been denied so long. Then I will take a day and you will take a day."

He shook his head. "It is yours," he said, "I have no right to take it from you."

"You will not take it from me," I said. "We will share it."

"Very well," he agreed. "But then let it be a day at a time, rather than my having it for an extended period at the start."

I saw that he was insistent, so said, "Agreed. But you will have it for the first day."

80

He smiled and a fresh out-cropping of tears glistened in his eyes.

I have thought often of that day, of the hunger in my friend's heart for the Word of God, of the deep satisfaction which came when once again he could sup from its bountiful provender.

And I have wondered about those careless children of God who take His Word so lightly. I wonder if they, too, would learn the pangs of real spiritual hunger if denied the voice of heaven for an extended period of time.

Why must the Word of God ever become commonplace? Is it because we have no need? Ah, my friend, our need is the greatest when we do not consciously hunger for the Book! When the regenerate heart strays into worldling ways so far as to be blinded by temporal glitter and thereby utterly misses the dazzling brilliance of eternal truth!

22

My thumb healed under the surveillance of the German doctor, sufficiently so that I was assigned back to work again. As in a previous camp, we pulled tree trunks out of the water, out of the icy water. Because of my weakened condition, I could only work two hours a day and I wondered how long my Russian captors would tolerate this dissipation of time and effort.

I spent much time in my barracks, resting. I utilized the long hours for meditation, for prayer and, on the days when it was allotted to me, study of the Word of God.

I enjoyed rich spiritual fellowship with my brother in Christ at the shoe repair shop. Not only with him, however. Because of his work, he delivered shoes to all areas of the camp and had thus encountered two other believers.

I helped him carry boxes of footwear and, as a result, met these two brethren. We established a rendezvous, the attic of a half-broken down building into which we would ascend by means of barrels and a pole. Here, at least once a week, the four of us met around the Word of God.

Surely no gathering of believers upon the face of the earth has ever cherished fellowship in Christ and inspiration from the Word more than did we! We would take turns reading from the Word of God. We would give testimonies of the Lord's goodness in our lives. We would share our prayer requests and lift them together to the Throne of Grace. We would sing the hymns of the faith, quietly — so as not to risk apprehension — but with great enthusiasm.

Winter's first heavy snow fell on the first day of October, and the temperature dropped to fifteen degrees below zero centigrade. The Russians issued us *malenkas* (felt boots) and *schappkas* (felt caps), and since it was much too cold now to work in the water, they assigned us to sifting gravel, laborious work done by hand.

But I felt no reason to complain, for my thumb was healing, and although my physical strength ebbed, we had a reasonably good supply of food and a warm place to sleep at night.

Speaking of food, I remember that my mess kit had many holes in it which I had to fix with clay. As you can understand, this was highly unsatisfactory.

One day at mess, a younger prisoner ridiculed me, saying, "Why don't you pray and ask God to give you another one?"

"I have been," I said.

He laughed, and others nearby laughed, also, and told what had been said to still others who joined in the merriment.

Just then a Jewish doctor came up to our table and, having been told nothing, saw my need and reported it to one of the officers. Immediately, I received another kit, made from a part of a rain gutter but of highly suitable material. I praised the Lord, and those who had ridiculed now looked silently at each other and at me.

Each day, except for an occasional tempering, the weather grew colder. And with the cold, my body continued to weaken until it became humanly impossible for me to go out with the work crews. I remained in the camp, feeling sure now that my presence as a parasite could not long be tolerated. I could not even get out to see my friend at the shoe repair shop, nor did he find opportunity to come to me. I confess my selfishness when I say that I was glad the Bible had last been in my custody. Otherwise, I would never have seen it again. For there was constant change in the camp, and during the early weeks of that winter, each of my brethren in Christ was moved elsewhere. At least I did not see them again.

The days were long . . . in spite of the fact that the sun rose late and set early . . . as I sat alone in the barracks. It was very cold, for we were not allowed to keep fire in the stove during the daylight hours. Why, I do not know, there being such an abundance of timber in the area, and the stronger men would have been willing to cut additional supplies.

One afternoon, unable to endure the cold, I lit a fire. Immediately, I was ordered to report to the German camp director, an Austrian who, like a number of the prisoners, had fallen into good favor with his captors.

After the evening meal, when all the prisoners stood in a line in the big square to be counted and given instructions for the next day, my name was called and I was summoned to the front.

I obeyed, trembling.

"You are placed under twenty-four hour arrest," I was told.

This meant that I would be placed in a hole outside, with no protection overhead, not so much as a cap or heavy outer garment.

I sat there alone in the darkness, looking at the sky above me, as the cold moved in like an invisible serpent, winding it's icy coils about my shivering frame. Knowing I could not possibly live through the night, I quietly committed myself to the Lord.

Because of my weakened condition, I fell asleep in spite of the cold. Then, about midnight, a hand gripped my shoulder. I looked up, awakening fully in that brief moment.

Four men from the barracks had ventured out to rescue me!

"Give us your hand," one of them whispered, "we'll pull you out."

"It is not wise," I said. "If they find that I am not here in the morning—"

"Don't let that concern you," the voice said. "You aren't the first one we've pulled out. The German is in charge of this, and he dare not give us too much trouble for fear of reprisal. Come."

They lifted me out, and I hurried quickly to my bed in the barracks.

There was a brisk fire in the stove, and it was warm, and my bed felt exceptionally soft, and I slept — a deep sleep of contentment and gratitude.

23

The days dragged into weeks, the weeks into months. Winter came in its fullness, cold and cruel and long.

My strength ebbed away at times to such alarming proportions that I do not know how I possibly survived. It was the grace of God! I remember finding a mirror in one of the buildings and looking into it horrified at the ghost of a man I saw there.

I lost weight. My hair silvered. My skin, which had been quite ruddy, turned to a sickly palor.

When the worst of winter came, entire weeks passed without our being able to venture out for work. We remained in our barracks, except to go to the mess hall for food. Mercifully, the Russians now permitted us to supply wood for our stove.

As winter progressed, we went to lectures held at a meeting hall off to one side of the camp where, hour after hour, we sat listening to Russian officers denounce the follies of capitalism and extoll the virtues of the communist way of life.

"The capitalistic world is asleep," I remember one lecturer saying, "while the giant of socialism rises to battle. The capitalists belittle our strength. They do not think we can rescue the laboring masses of the world from the hardships which have been imposed upon them.

"But the next decade shall see miracles. Not miracles from the sky, for the God of the capitalistic religionists is dead, if indeed He ever existed. But miracles shall rise from the earth, wrought by the hands of men dedicated to the communist faith. Men set free to find their highest potentialities.

"The capitalists do not believe this, but Russia shall soon rule the world. In science. In government. In military might. And, most important of all, in helping men discover the true meaning of life."

This particular lecturer received a considerable amount of discussion among the men in my barracks. Most of them laughed, relating example after example of Russian backwardness.

"These teachers are nothing but parrots!" I remember a prisoner saying. He had graduated from one of Germany's leading universities. "What do they know about science? What do they know about government? What do they know about anything?"

"Germany would have had them on their knees in a month, if it had not been that America supplied the Soviets with weapons and military guidance," said another.

A man near me, grown old before his time in the cold crucible of Siberia, mumbled, "America saved Russia from oblivion, and now the Russians boast that they will wipe the capitalists off from the face of the earth."

"Ho!" one of the younger men laughed at this. "Let Russia make one false move, and the Americans will give them the full dose of what was sampled at Hiroshima and Nagasaki!"

Another young man came over to my mat and kicked my foot lightly. "What do you predict *Herr Dokter?* You have your head in the clouds! What do the angels say about all this?"

The men laughed . . . some of them . . . and I preferred to keep silent.

"Tell us," someone shouted from across the barracks. "What does God say?"

I lifted to my elbow. "God has once spoken, through His Word, and He need say no more. In the New Testament, it is written, *This know also, that in the last days perilous times shall come. For men shall be lovers of their own selves, covetous, proud, blasphemous . . . evil men and seducers shall wax worse, deceiving, and being deceived.* The ways of evil shall reach great pinacles of success, but God will always be far above the greatest attainment, and when man has had his day, God shall have His."

Somehow, the Holy Spirit used that faltering comment, bringing a strange hush upon the entire barracks. I heard a few mumblings, a subdued laugh in the distance, but otherwise all was quiet.

I sat up, although my head pounded, and my body trembled from weakness. "Be sure of this, comrades!" I proclaimed boldly. "God is in His heaven, although all may not be right with the world. *Be not deceived: God is not mocked: for whatsoever a man soweth, that shall he also reap. For he that soweth to his flesh shall of the flesh reap corruption; but he that soweth to the Spirit shall of the Spirit reap life everlasting.* It is not what happens to the world or to any nation within the world that is important. It is what happens to your eternal soul. And the destiny of your soul is in your hands.

"Jesus said: *Come unto me all ye that labour and are heavy laden, and I will give you rest . . . Him that cometh unto Me, I will in no wise cast out . . . Verily, verily, I say unto you, He that heareth my Word, and believeth on Him that sent me, hath everlasting life, and shall not come into condemnation; but is passed from death unto life."*

I lay back upon my resting place. Darkness and silence permeated every corner of the barracks. Outside, the wind rose with blustering intensity. Home and loved ones were far away.

But in my heart, there was radiance . . . there was peace.

24

Winter in Siberia!

Snow fell, not by inches but by feet. And the wind came in like an evil presence, seeking out those whom it might destroy. Why I did not perish from the cold, I shall never know. The temperature plunged to sixty degrees below zero, and it was impossible to walk full-face into the wind. One could as easily breathe fire!

While out on work detail, many of the prisoners perished from exposure. Sometimes they would drop in their tracks, freezing to death on the spot. Among ourselves, we called it the "polar plague." Many of our heartiest men perished.

The head of my work detail, a fellow prisoner, realized my physical condition, and arranged excuses for me, whenever possible, to work among the buildings. I felt like kissing his feet. Although he was an unbeliever to whom I had often witnessed in vain, I feel confident he was guided by Almighty God.

Mercifully, the Russians allowed us additional portions of food, most of it hot. And so long as we provided necessary lumber for firewood, we were permitted to have heat in the barracks. Yet on the cold, cold nights, even though the stove burned red-hot at one side of the barracks, the corners of the building became lined with frost from our breath. We moved our mats together, keeping each other warm like animals.

The morale of the men dropped to its lowest ebb. Many of them became like automatons — their faces blank, their eyes fixed on nothingness. Some took their own lives.

I remember one night, when we sat huddled about the fire as one of the most desperate storms of the winter howled outside.

One of the men began talking about his wife. I suppose it would seem obscene to you, were I to give the details of what he said, but had you been there, had your mind been conditioned as was ours, you would have understood.

"I loved that woman!" he screamed. "Do you hear me? I never loved another!"

He leaped to his feet, ran over to the door. We watched him. No one offered so much as a restraining hand.

He stood at the door for a moment and released a flow of blasphemy such as I hope never again to hear. "I can't stand it!" he screamed. "I can't stand it!" Then, opening the door, he ran out into the storm, never to be seen again.

One of our men got up and slowly walked over and closed the door. No one spoke. Those were dark days, and even darker nights, and my own soul tottered at the verge of despondency.

Yet God was merciful.

Toward the end of February, when I wondered how I could possibly endure another week, mail came in from the west. With it was a letter from my wife! I must have read it five hundred times! I read it until it wore thin in my hands!

My dearest husband,
We are in reasonable health, well cared for, and con-

fident in our hearts that, no matter where you are, you shall some day return to us. Love,
(Signed)

Yes, there is winter. There is heartache. There is man's inhumanity to man. But so long as there is love, the human spirit can go on and on.

25

Spring came, as Siberia knows spring. Snow lingered on the ground, and fell occasionally from the skies, and at nights it would freeze, but the deep cold had gone.

Somehow, the cold of winter had arrested my dystrophy. But I was weak, horribly weak, and the skin lay on my bones like a piece of silk thrown over a skeleton. So you can imagine my joy when, that spring, word came that two thousand POW's would be returned to Germany. My name appeared among them!

One morning we heard the chugging of a freight train, as it backed a line of cars along the spur which lead to our camp. We were like little boys, those in my barracks, for all of us had been chosen to make the trip home. Men wept unashamedly, I among them.

Together with some thirty comrades, I was dispatched to a detail sent to get the train in order. It had come through a considerable amount of snow, which we had to remove. Also, we assembled a *goulasch-cannon*—an oven on board one of the freight cars, to be used in preparing food.

We sang as we worked, songs of the homeland, songs of childhood. I led in the singing of Luther's *A Mighty Fortress*, and the men joined in like a concert chorale. We returned late that afternoon to camp, light of foot in anticipation of the coming morning when we would begin the homeward journey.

No one could sleep that night. We laughed and chattered, and told each other about our home and loved ones. It seemed the night would never pass.

At dawn everyone was up and dressed. A Russian officer came, ordered us to get in line. There, one by one, the name was called of each man to make the trip back to Germany. Two thousand names were called. Two thousand men, their destination Germany.

But not my name!

Why? During the time my comrades and I had gone to prepare the train, the others had been registered. Because our names had not been included, we were left behind.

I was stunned. My mind seemed not to function, remaining fixed on but one thought, the fact that I would not be returning to my loved ones. I did not speak. I did not weep.

"Sorry, Comrade," I remember hearing some of the men say. I do not recall making any reply.

"I will get word to your wife," another said.

Those to be liberated marched out of the camp and off to the railroad tracks, their feet crunching like mockery upon the snow-covered ground. I watched them go and as the train at last pulled away, it was like attending one's own funeral. At least for that moment, I lost hope of ever seeing my loved ones again.

We watched until the train disappeared in the distance. We listened, until the last chug of the engine, the last clatter of the wheels on the rails, was lost in the awful Siberian stillness.

That night, in a camp all but deserted, two of those left behind took their lives. I think that, were it not for God's watch-care upon my soul, I might have done the same.

Despair? Yes, I know despair! Yet . . . in that strange mystic reality which is the heritage of every believer . . . I seemed to hear the voice of God deep in my heart, saying: "Fret not, my child. There is yet work for thee to do."

And there was work for me to do. Other prisoners came in, and I realized that here were men needing to know my Saviour. I grew bold in my witness, and soon the Russian officers learned that I not only had a Bible, which I read, but that I was giving it to others to read.

One night, as I was about to retire, one of the officers came.

"You are the man who has a copy of the Bible!" he snapped. "Give it to me!"

With a trembling hand, I gave the Book to him.

As I watched him leave, I felt an even greater horror than had come upon me when I watched the departure of the train that was to have taken me back to my loved ones. Precious though the Word of God had been to me, I did not until that moment realize its full worth to my soul!

I thanked God that I had laid store so much of it in my heart. Because of my weakened condition, my memory seemed to fail at times, and yet the Word of God remained like a lucid voice in my heart. But I wanted my Bible back again, and I prayed fervently that God would somehow make this possible.

The next day, I was summoned before several Russian officers. There, within easy reach if I had dared to pick it up, lay my Bible!

One of the officers, checking a file card, spoke my name. "This is your copy of the Bible?" he asked.

"It is," I told him.

He looked at me for a moment, his eyes burning like two brands. Again he spoke my name. "You could use more food, and more suitable working conditions."

I said nothing.

"You may have these, you may have them in considerable abundance . . ." He picked up my Bible, held it menacingly in his hands. ". . . if you will deny that you hold any allegiance to this Book!"

I did not speak. I did not know what to say. *Lord God of heaven*, I prayed silently, *give me courage!*

"Will you deny such allegiance?" the officer asked.

"I could have done that under Hitler," I told him, surprised at the words which fell from my lips.

Apparently my reply was not expected, and the men conferred among themselves in Russian. Then the officer, who had been thumbing through the Bible, hurled it onto the table. It fell within easy reach of my hands.

I hesitated a moment. Slowly, I picked up the Book, and held it firmly within my hands.

Once more my name was spoken. "You are hereby sentenced to the punishment squad!"

I was then turned over to a lesser officer, who led me away. Miraculously, I held the Bible in my hand. No one took it from me. I felt like Daniel, in a den of lions whose mouths had been closed by the power of Almighty God!

26

Together with some other prisoners, who had received sentences like mine, I marched for ten hours to the punishment camp! How I was physically able to do this, I can never know, except that I am sure God sustained me.

"What will it be like?" I whispered to one of the men, as we marched.

"From what I have heard," he said, "it will be hell! Why were you sentenced?" When I told him, he scoffed, "You fool!" and would not speak with me further.

I scrutinized the other men in our group — a motley crowd, indeed. Faces drawn, eyes aflame. I wondered about the sanity of many of them. There were, of course, some like myself who, for an infraction displeasing to the Russians, had been sentenced.

One of these latter said to me, "This is the beginning of the end, Comrade."

"What do you mean?" I asked.

"Precisely what I said."

A guard drifted back beside us, snapped, *"Paschly!"*

I took care not to enter into any further conversation, it being obviously frowned upon by our captors. I needed to conserve my strength, as — mile after mile — we trudged over the jagged trail. Mile after mile and hour after hour.

Perhaps I might have become fearful of the prediction that this was allegedly the beginning of the end, except the Lord had endowed me with a special portion of physical strength and, with it, the renewed conviction that my destiny was secure in Him.

We reached the camp by nightfall and were placed in a heavily guarded hut with nothing but earth floor. Completely exhausted, however, I lay down and fell asleep.

I had a beautiful dream, in which it seemed the Lord Himself came and spoke to me, spoke my name. "A new commando will be formed," He said. "It will be for volunteers. Join it."

We were awakened at five the next morning and were told that a commando was being formed to work in the woods. Anyone who wished might volunteer.

The men glanced warily at each other, suspecting an even greater fate should they volunteer their services. But, remembering my dream, I stepped willingly forward. Several others joined me.

This, too, was by the grace of God. For before we left the camp, for a five hour march into the woods, I heard enough to know what my lot would have been had I remained there. The punishment camp was made up mostly of SS men and prisoners who had been exceedingly difficult to handle. There was no mercy.

The leader of the group with which I had volunteered had no more than taken us to our new camp, when he came to me and mentioned my bad condition. I was then in rags, and he brought me a jacket which, he said quite frankly, had been taken from the body of a man who died the day before. He assigned me to eight days of light work, together with a special diet of better food. "*Donka!*" I exclaimed. "*Donka!*" He smiled.

Shortly after the eight days was up, we moved on to a new camp, one which included a hospital section. I marvelled at the evidence of God's guidance, for my condition now made it imperative that I be placed in the hospital.

The camp was something of a village, and the hospital appeared to be in an abandoned theatre. There was fancy ornamentation, and the building was laid out in a semi-circle.

On the main floor lay some five hundred wounded Germans, on the balcony several hundred Hungarians. I lay in almost the direct center of the main floor, my duffle bag, containing all of my belongings, including my Bible, at my side.

I wanted to read it but, to be very frank, I had hesitated about establishing my testimony as a Christian. Should I read the Bible and risk the possibility of persecution on the part of my captors? Not to mention the scorn of some of the prisoners? In all my tenure as a prisoner, I had not known such comfort as that now afforded me. The human quest is for comfort, and I deliberated long the peril of losing it should I manifest openly my Christian witness.

For several minutes, doubt besieged my soul. I prayed, earnestly asking God for strength, and He gave me victory. I took out the Bible and began reading.

But I had scarcely opened it, when a German army doctor, a major, came up to me. "The Holy Scriptures!" he exclaimed. "God's Word! All these years during the war, and now as a prisoner, I have wanted to read it! May I borrow it!"

I offered it to him, much as I wanted to keep it for myself! "I am on the night shift," he said. "I will come and get it while you sleep, and return it to you in the morning."

He left and, my heart warm, I began reading again.

Soon another German POW, serving as a medic, came to me, his reaction almost identical to that of the doctor. Not only did these two want to read my Bible, but a number of the patients asked for permission to see it, so many, in fact, that the time came when I had to make out a chart covering the hours of the day, assigning the time when various ones could read my precious volume.

I do not in the least exaggerate when I say that the entire attitude of that hospital changed. Even the Russian officials took notice of it, apparently with pleasure, and I have often wondered if it set any of them thinking.

Men had been phlegmatic, without hope, with little of any desire to get well. But now this changed. The men began offering thanks to God before meals, even the Hungarians in the balcony.

It was almost as though we were no longer prisoners.

27

After my long tenure in the hospital, I received a medical discharge and was taken, together with two or three hundred other men, to the railroad siding, where we were loaded onto freight cars.

"I think we are being sent back to Germany!" one man said. And his words sprung hope into all of our hearts. We did not mind the fact that there was only a small stove in the car. We did not mind the jerking and jostling of the train, as it moved laboriously on its way. We did not mind the lack of food. We were going home!

Late one night—it must have been well beyond midnight — the train came to a stop. We thought nothing of it, for there had been long delays both by day and at night. I, as a matter of fact, fell asleep, being better able to do so when the train stood still than when in movement, because of the hard floor.

Suddenly, I awakened to a gust of cold air and the blinding gleam of a search light.

Paschly!" a guard called in familiar command.

Instantly, we all jumped to our feet, and, at the guard's command, detrained. We stood by companies — each freight car's passengers being considered a company — and I soon learned that, in the course of our travel, we had added several hundred additional POW's to our number.

In the faint light of the moon, I could make out that we were again in heavily wooded area. As to any other identity of our location, I couldn't be sure. To this day I am not sure. I presume, however, that we were either within the fringe of Russia itself, or else in a more habitable area of Siberia, for I subsequently learned that a small village lay but a short distance from our camp.

We stood for an hour there in the darkness, in the bitter cold. I trembled from chill until I feared that I might have to sit down, not knowing how such an act might be taken by my captors. I prayed earnestly for strength, for in spite of my weakness, optimism throbbed through my body like a hidden strength. With all my heart, I believed we were being processed for return to Germany!

At last, the command came for us to march, and we made our way to a camp a distance of about a mile from the railroad tracks.

"Who says we're returning to Germany?" I heard one man mumble nearby.

"Have you been returned before?" someone asked.

"What do you mean?"

"They surely have an embarkation center, from which prisoners-of-war are processed before being returned to their native land."

The gist of this conversation spread quickly among the prisoners, even though we were marching, and quickened the step of many a homesick man. Including my own!

Upon reaching the camp, we were once more assembled into the same groups in which we had traveled and required to stand for a considerable length of time. I seemed to have fallen heir to a hidden strength, for I did not tire now. Nor did I tremble from the cold. My thoughts were only of home, of my beloved wife and children, and of the fact that — so far as I could ascertain — I would soon be with them.

In the moonlight, to which my eyes had now become fully accustomed, I made out that we were in a camp quite different from where we had been before. Different, that is, in that it seemed to be of more durable construction.

"This is an abandoned training camp of the Russian army," I heard a man say. Where he got the information, I did not know, but it later proved to be correct.

"Then the war certainly must be over," said another man. We had, of course, been told that it was, but no one was sure. "Otherwise," the man continued, "this camp would be in use by the Russians."

A pleasant thought came to my mind. Because of the lectures we had heard, regarding the alleged rising strength of the Russian nation, I had supposed that a strongly militaristic program was being maintained. The fact of this abandoned camp led me to believe that perhaps this was not so.

Could it be that, even in so wicked a world, men had at last realized the utter folly of war, the fact that no one really could win? It was, of course, wishful thinking, but such thoughts did go through my mind.

At last—after a long period of waiting; how long, I can only surmise — we were assigned to barracks. To these we went immediately, being instructed to remove all of our clothes for thorough examination.

"Not some more of those women doctors!" one man mumbled with a half-laugh.

By now we had learned that seventy per cent of the medical doctors in Russia are women, the practice of medicine not being held in esteem as it is in other countries of the

97

world. A doctor, by Russian standards, had a value rating similar to that of a foreman in a factory.

To my own relief, there was no medical examination. But, instead, Russian guards came in and meticulously went through all our belongings. They examined everything — our pockets, the seams of our coats, even the natural recesses of our bodies. I prayed earnestly, as a guard went through my rucksack, wondering if the presence of my Bible might hinder my return to Germany. It was a case of mixed emotions, to be sure, but once again the Lord gave me victory. For I knew, deep in my heart, that if the presence of my Bible did require my remaining longer a prisoner, it was only so that I could more effectively bear witness to those who otherwise would not hear of my Blessed Lord.

The guard did examine my Bible momentarily, but seemed to attach no significance to it, and tossed it back into my rucksack. I wondered if he had never seen a Bible before and considered it no more than some German novel I happened to have with me. As had happened times before, my heart lifted silent paeans of praise to my Heavenly Father for permitting me to keep His Word with me!

At last the guards left and we quickly put on our clothes, for there was only a small fire in the heater that warmed the barracks. I stretched out on a cot to await further developments and fell asleep.

It seemed, however, that I slept only a moment when, opening my eyes, I found that day had fully come. More than that, the barracks was empty. I jumped to my feet and, looking out of a window near by, saw the men marching away from camp.

Frantic, I hurried outside and, not wishing to be disciplined for tardiness, kept to some undergrowth along the road, even though it meant tramping through rather heavy snow, until I came up to the tail of the line. Imagine my relief when I discovered that there was my contingent.

"Where are we marching?" I asked one of my comrades.
"To the train."

"Why?"

"Why? Don't you even know where you're going?"

"Back to Germany?" I asked wistfully.

"Back to Germany," came the reply.

Somewhere in the distance — from where, it did not matter — I heard music. Vast chorale and orchestra in a rising crescendo that enveloped the entire countryside. The "Hallelujah Chorus," the "Grand March," and the "Doxology."

We marched quickly to the railroad tracks and, as though we needed no instructions, were placed on board. In only a matter of moments, the train began to move.

And it was not box cars, but passenger coaches almost identical to those used in Germany. And they were warm, delightfully so.

"We are being returned to Germany, aren't we?" I asked a man sitting across from me. He nodded, but I saw a strange fear in his eyes.

I looked out the window, watched the countryside fly by like some strange unbelievable fantasy. It was hypnotic and I sat there for what seemed an eternity until, suddenly, the most amazing thing happened. The train pulled into the railroad station of my home town in Germany! And there, eagerly waiting on the platform, stood my wife and children!

I discovered something else, too. Once again, I was alone. Completely unnoticed by me, all of the other men had gone from the train. I rapped on the window, calling my wife's name, but she did not see me. And then, to my horror, the train began to move. I jumped to my feet, and ran toward the exit.

"Hilde! Hilde!" I screamed at the top of my voice.

Suddenly a man appeared, at first blocking my way in the train and then, by some weird transition, bending over me. "You fool! Do you want to get us all in trouble?"

It took me only a moment to realize what had taken place. I had been dreaming. I was still in the prison camp to which we had been moved, the camp where I was to spend the next two years!

28

The excruciating reality of what had happened came slowly upon all of us. For several days, many of the men clung to the conviction that we were being processed for return to Germany. "How do we know that it is anything else?" they reasoned. "Those who have been returned before may have gone through periods of detention the same as we are."

But as the days passed slowly, becoming weeks, then a month and more, hope died in our hearts.

If you have ever gone through great tragedy, the kind of disappointment that sears the very soul, you know that, in looking back, one finds vast periods of total blankness. This is the mercy of the human frame, by which the mind refuses to retain many details of those happenings which, although they may be very important in our lives, bring sorrow.

It was this way for me.

We were again assigned to logging operations, I presume to supply the vast need for timber in a Russia which I have since learned is going through a period of unprecedented awakening. My body had wasted to the stature and strength of an old man. Yet day after day, somehow, I plodded with my contingent out to the forest.

Because of my obvious physical condition, I was not asked to handle the saw or the ax. I did more menial tasks. Running errands. Keeping tabulations. As I say, much of it is completely blank to me. Mercifully blank.

I do remember that men died. I remember that there were those who revolted against the oppressor and were then seen no more. In whatever manner you could call this joking, for it was certainly not a jest in the strictest sense of the word, we came to speak of those who disappeared as having "gone on vacation" or "returned early to Germany."

Desperately, I clung to the sustenance of God's eternal Word — many times not for any other reason but to cling to whatever personal sanity I might have, concerned lest I become totally irrational. I remember how I would sit for hours at a time, looking at the Bible. I tried desperately to read, yet time after time my thoughts would wander, the page would become blurred, and my mind would devote itself to fantasies which, once I gripped reality again, left me bewildered and ashamed.

Ashamed?

Yes, I will be honest with you. There is no point in being otherwise. Although, believe me, there is much of my story which I shall leave unrecorded along with those blank periods of which even I know neither the basic occurrences nor the details.

I will tell you, however, that Satan besieged my soul during those months of continuance as a prisoner of the Soviet Union. There came periods of horrible doubt, when questioning my own salvation became a minor thing as compared to doubts as to the validity of the Bible, doubts as to the efficacy of the atonement, even doubts as to the existence of God Himself.

We continued to be subjected to indoctrination lectures by Russian officers. I remember how I would find myself listening in rapt attention to the masterful flow of words, the logic of the communist line. And I remember how we would discuss these matters back in the barracks.

"Maybe it makes sense," one man said, coming to me privately. "I thought I believed the Bible the way you do. I thought I believed in God. But maybe the Russians are trying to show us mercy. Maybe there is no God. Maybe the Bible is nothing but a book of myths. Maybe communism is the answer to the world's need. Maybe the communists have found this kind of subjection the best way to bring a man to his senses."

I remember how I sat and stared at that man, how I followed him as he got up and walked away to another section

101

of the barracks. I remember how I reasoned in my mind, trying to argue against my own faith in support of the points he had expressed.

Then I remember how I snatched my Bible from my rucksack, how I opened it and feverishly searched the Word of God for bulwark to sustain my faith, how I unashamedly wept as I came to passage after passage in which God assured us that in this world we can expect tribulation but to be of good cheer because He has overcome the world.

Yes, I had known temptation and heartache prior to my becoming a prisoner of the Russians. I had come to what I had considered times of great testing of my faith. But, looking back, I know that those times were as nothing compared to the satanic bombardments which besieged my soul during those weeks and months.

The most difficult of all was witnessing. For weeks at a time, I did not witness. I couldn't. Then, getting hold of myself, I tried once more to give testimony to my faith in Christ.

"You don't believe a word you're saying," one man told me. He looked squarely in my eye. "You are clinging to religious convictions that have long become outmoded in your thinking. You know it. Sure, you could believe in God and that Book and the other things you talk about when life was normal. But now . . . now it is different. It is in your eyes, Comrade. It is in your voice. You don't believe what you're saying to me. Why don't you be honest and admit it?"

We looked at each other for a long, long moment. And deep in my heart, like the voice of a great thunder, came such questions as I had never faced before. *Do you believe in God? Do you believe that in your hands you hold the immutable, irrefutable, eternal Word of the Almighty? Do you believe that Jesus Christ was, in every respect, what He claimed to be, the Son of God, and God the Son? Do you believe that when He died on the Cross, He bore there the sins of the whole world, and that, by faith in Him, any man*

*can be eternally safe? Do you believe these things? Do you
believe them?*

I remember the tears rolling down my cheeks, as I silently
cried out to my Saviour for mercy and strength. Mercy to
forgive my questionings. Strength to carry me through victor-
iously.

"Be honest, Comrade!" the man snarled at me. "Be honest! Do you believe these things?"

"Yes," I whispered, and even I could hear the new ring of
sincerity in my voice. "I believe it! I believe every word!"

29

I remember that summer came, such as there was to summer, and that before the end of August, the silver birch
leaves turned a pale yellow and brown, until they became
like silent ghosts standing among the green pine. I remember how the wind came and tore the leaves from the decidu-
ous branches, scattering them across the ground. I remember
that there was no rain, nothing to rot the leaves, and that
they lay beautiful and immaculate upon the ground until, late
in September, the first snow fell.

Even though we had seen winter come before, we were all
horrified to be reminded of the fact that it came so early.

With winter came cold. Most of us grew beards, not only
because of the lack of soap and razors, but as a bulwark
against the biting winds which swept down upon us. We
were under quite limited surveillance in this new camp, but
it made little difference. Few if any gave so much as a
thought to running away. I am sure the Russians had long
before learned that, once passing through a winter in this
part of the world, no man in his right mind would attempt
escape.

The effects of malnutrition began to manifest themselves more apparently than ever before. Many of us suffered from toothache, because the unbalanced diet caused the fillings to be lost from our teeth, not to mention new cavities which appeared. Yellow, purulent sores broke out on our skin, plus the nagging listlessness that plagues those who do not get sufficient food.

I must be honest in regard to the Russians. I do not believe they were purposely giving us inadequate food. I think perhaps the provender we received was, in some measure at least, similar to that available to the poorer classes of Russia. I am sure that much of our deprivation in the prison camps was due to the very fact of a low standard of living in all of Russia.

From the attitude of our guards, one could see that they felt we were being extended somewhat normal treatment. Except for egress from their country during actual fighting, when no one can view another in his natural habitat, these men had perhaps no concept of the way of life previously enjoyed by their captives.

The whole history of the Russian people is, of course, one of separation from the world. There has always been the endless, desolate steppe, buried in snow half the time and thus being, itself, a natural obstacle in the path of the foreign invader. The Russian people are caught in the necessitating limitations of their privacy — ill-equipped with modern techniques to fight the summer heat and drought, the winter's cold and snow. And, of course, there has always been poverty, aggravated by war after war in the making of which the people had no voice. There has been the oppressive rule from above, the dictatorship by men of the Kremlin whether they be czars or commissars who, themselves, by reason of their own insecurity, imposed great hardships upon their subjects.

For centuries, troops have guarded the frontiers of Russia. The Russian people, during the years, have learned to distrust foreigners. With the exception of Peter the Great —

who sought something in the way of fraternization with the Western World—Russian rulers have endeavored to keep the people of their country in a state of isolation.

And, of course, the modern Iron Curtain, forged by Joseph Stalin, embodies all of the elements of this innate isolationism.

So, as I said before, I presume our guards, for the most part, sincerely believed we were being treated properly. In their opinion, we were prisoners, thus not entitled to many civil benefits, but we were, nonetheless, considered as human beings.

It was the imprisonment itself which, in my opinion, showed either an outright disregard for human decency or a lack of the most basic understanding of the human personality.

Three years I was a prisoner of the Russians. Why? I appeared before no tribunal. I had committed no wrong other than serving my country. Why then this imprisonment? I do not know the answer. It was never offered to me.

Was it to somehow make restitution for the havoc the German army had wrecked upon Russia itself? Were we in that sense of the word criminals? Or was it the Machiavellian concepts of communism itself? If the country needed raw materials, such as lumber and coal, and there were not enough of the populace itself to be subjected to the hardships required in securing these raw materials, then perhaps the very philosophy of communism was such that it became right to inflict wrong upon innocent beings such as ourselves.

Observers of the Russian scene insist that the utilization of slave labor has long been considered a legitimate *modus operandi* in the expansion of the communist cause. For years, slave labor camps have existed in Siberia. While I was not subjected to one which held Russian citizens, I am told that thousands and thousands of them are held in camps just as we, German prisoners-of-war, were held. When more labor is needed, the Kremlin need only call for a purge of additional "undesirable" citizens to be shipped into Siberia.

One writer tells of a conversation with a Soviet citizen, who was reported to have said: "Because of the purges, there is not so much as one Russian citizen who has not either himself been locked up, or has had some member of his relation sent to a concentration camp."

Possibly at the time I was held prisoner, when the communist party was once more winning its way back into favor after the long years of war, it was considered best not to "recruit" from among the citizenry. Perhaps that was why I had to spend three long years as a laborer, even when my physical strength was such that I could do little beyond menial tasks. I do not know.

30

Those next two winters were long and hard. I could not have survived them, but for the grace of God, for I shrank to the stature and weight of an adolescent boy.

The one winter was exceptionally hard, so severe that weeks passed without any work being done in the forests. Consequently, the Russians cut our rations. The *klepp* became almost impalatable, and was served to us in such sparse quantities that at meal times we often played childishly with it, cutting it into small squares, then cubes, then minute slices, just to make it seem more. Sometimes it took as much as an hour to eat one slice of bread!

Many of our comrades died, especially when the winter came in its fullest force, but also as spring came on, when those who had been weakened by the long cold would succumb to epidemics which swept through the camp.

The Lord worked a wonderful miracle for me, in that I was privileged to spend time with many of my comrades during their last hours. More than once, in the dead of night, someone would come and awaken me. On one occasion, at least, it was a Russian guard who came. I would be hurried to the hospital barracks, to stand at the side of a German prisoner spending his last moments upon earth.

I know that many Christians take small stock in what has come to be known as "death-bed conversions" but I am not quite sure I can agree. Many times, I stood with the Word of God in hand at the side of a dying prisoner and saw the very light of heaven gleam upon his face as, through the unction of the Holy Spirit, I was able to get across to him the glorious reality of God's provision for eternal salvation.

Oh, I continued to face ridicule for my Christian witness. But I sometimes wonder if a witness is valid for Christ unless it does become subjected to some ridicule. But, for the most part, there was respect on the part of the men and, with nothing whatsoever in the way of a chaplaincy among us, I came to be known as the spiritual teacher.

At times, the Russians permitted me to accompany to the last resting place the bodies of those who died. The corpse would be laid on a couple of boards, then carried—as on a litter — by two long poles. As we made our way to the little burying plot, those who had known the deceased would stand at quiet attention, watching. Clearly written upon the face of every man was the question: "Which of us will be next?"

Each body would be placed naked into the ground, so as to conserve each garment, no matter how worn. Branches from the fir trees would be laid on the body, and then the earth.

I was allowed to offer a brief prayer, although I could not read from the Bible, and then we would make our way back to the camp. It happened many times.

The deceased would be identified by a wooden pole, containing his name and serial number. That very first winter in this new camp, however, when the snow was so deep that we sometimes waded to the waist, these poles disappeared for use as firewood, and thus would go the last identifica-

107

tion of the remains of someone who, like myself, had loved ones longing for his return.

The supply of food grew less and less, until we reached the point where it seemed altogether possible that we might face actual starvation. I think perhaps we might not have minded, had food been cut off entirely, for surely quick starvation, terrible as it may be, is more merciful than constant pangs of hunger, growing ever greater as the supply of food becomes less and less.

31

Hunger!

It is like a living thing, like a sickness, like a curse. It has its beginning in the stomach, but it is most felt in the mind. Some of our men suffered from hallucinations and would rush madly about the barracks pretending to be gulping mouthfuls of food! It was a pathetic sight, as you can well imagine. Many of the prisoners broke mentally, and had to be removed — where to, I do not know — and hunger, coupled with loneliness and uncertainty, must surely have brought on a major portion of these break-downs.

I was assigned to a detail which brought me frequently into the little village near our camp. While I realized the danger of such procedure, and certainly felt every measure of the deep humiliation to which it subjected me, I actually went on many occasions from door to door, begging for so much as a morsel of food. And the people were merciful, for while they had no abundance to supply their own needs, many times I was given food from the very pots out of which they were cooking their meals. Because of my great physical weakness, I would have perished had it not been for food supplied in this manner.

Entering the home of any of the Russian people was strictly forbidden — and would have, in all probability, been punishable by death — but several times I entered the homes of those who extended to me the radiance of their hearts. God bless them! How I wish I could have spoken to them, to have told them of my gratitude and to have shared with them the Food they so desperately needed, the blessed Bread of Life!

In one home, I met an old man who had a radiance in his eyes that led me to believe he knew my Saviour. For it is true, as I trust you've experienced, that there is something about God's children which gives them away, especially when you find them in a setting of such total darkness.

Through sign language, I was able to make known to this man that I, too, was a believer. I shall never forget the joy that flooded his countenance.

He took me into another room, carefully closed the shutters lest anyone see from the outside, and then, using an oil lamp, he removed some boards from a creaking stairway. Here he had hidden parts of an old hymnal, parts of a Bible and some pamphlets which I made out to be Gospel tracts in the Russian language.

I wept, and so did he!

I could not speak to him and he could not speak to me, but as brothers in Christ, we knelt together and prayed. He prayed first, in his own tongue, and my heart surged with spiritual excitement as, time after time, I heard him utter what I knew to be the Russian equivalent of Jesus Christ our Saviour and Lord!

He poured from his heart such a cry to heaven as I have seldom heard before, not a cry of anguish, so far as I could determine, but one of gratitude and praise.

And then I prayed. I thanked God for the reality of salvation, for the great miracle of true Christian brotherhood through the blood of Jesus Christ, for the love that is shed abroad in the heart of every believer through the indwelling presence of the Holy Spirit. As I prayed, this brother put his arm around me, clutching me close to himself.

When I left, he gestured with his hands, indicating that he wanted me to come back again. This I did about a week later, to be met at the door by the dear brother himself. But there was panic in his eyes and, again using his hands, he made it clear it would not be possible for him to permit me into his house. He could not tell me why, but apparently someone knew of our having been together and had at least threatened to report the incident were it to occur again.

We stood there for a moment, looking at each other. Then he pressed into my hand a piece of soup meat and three onions — both of them nothing short of delicacies! — and motioned for me to leave. I never saw him again, but I shall. Someday, together with multitudes of redeemed ones from every nation of earth, I shall stand before the One who alone is worthy of our praise!

God also arranged so that I was assigned to work which involved transporting butter from a nearby farm to the railroad train, for transportation to market. Here again I was shown mercy by the Russian people. The farmer, a kind little man, did not so much as suggest that either I or the one or two men who would usually be with me should come to his house for food. But he always arranged to leave several pats of butter outside the containers. These we would eat ravenously, as we made our way to the railroad tracks.

There was the bark of one of the trees that we had been eating, to combat hunger, and I remember how palatable it tasted one day as we stopped for a moment, secured some of the bark, and spread it thickly with rich butter!

One of the Russian officers had a dog in the camp. On it's collar, printed in German, he had placed a tag which read: "Do not harm." Nonetheless, the dog disappeared, having provided a meal for some prisoners who found the little animal when he had strayed too far from his master.

Not only did we have problems with food, but also with sanitation. I could never quite understand how the Russian

Army used this area as a camp, since the supply of water seemed to be limited. Maybe it was not limited at all, but only deprived from us as part of our punishment. At any rate, we were permitted to take baths no more than three times a year, the common decency of allowing a man to wash his hands before eating unheard of. This proved all the more exasperating since rodents literally overran the camp.

And then when summer came, and with it a highly stepped-up program of work which involved ten days in the forest to one day of rest, mosquitoes moved in like a plague. They got into our eyes, into our nostrils, and we would work hours at a time with the carniverous creatures feasting upon us in such abundance it became useless to try to fight them away.

"If at least the mice ate the mosquitoes or the mosquitoes ate mice, it wouldn't be so bad!" one of our men grumbled.

But, all praise to His name, my God had seen me once-and-for-all through the valley of discouragement. Now, no matter how hard the lot might be, I had peace and victory in my heart. His Word became more and more precious to me, and He gave me opportunity after opportunity to speak to my comrades about their soul's salvation. Many of them professed to find Christ as their Saviour. How many of these remained true to their profession, I do not know, but I thank God for the opportunities I had for witness.

Yes, God had taught me that the life of victory can be the norm — not the abnormal — for the believer. Bereft of life's most commonplace comforts, subjected to the constant uncertainty of the future, given no promise of any kind as to ever again enjoying the way of life I had once known, I learned to completely trust in the Lord.

Siberia was a hard experience but it was also a good one.

Yes, I had learned to trust my God, but this did not obliterate my desire again to be reunited with my loved ones. I praised Him that, although during my three years imprisonment the Russians only permitted me on six occasions to write to my wife — and then only to send a post card — the fact that I did have contact with her did much to heighten my spirits. On one occasion, she took a picture of our children, stitched it to the back of a post card, and sent it to me. The censors, of course, severed the picture sufficiently to determine whether or not any message had been hidden, but eventually it got to me. It blessed my soul!

So far as we could tell, mail was censored three times. Anything the Russians did not want us to read would be clipped out, not merely blacked over. Of course, if anything too objectionable was found, I suppose that the correspondence was destroyed completely. We had no way of knowing.

One of our men, although he had written faithfully whenever we were given the opportunity, had received no word from home. He became greatly despondent, and, one morning following a day of unusual discouragement, he did not answer roll call. We found him dead. Suicide.

That same evening, at mail call, a letter came from his wife . . . from a refugee camp.

32

There is much more I could tell you, much more. Of suffering. Of despondency. Of the toll despair takes upon the lives of human kind. But my purpose in relating this story has not been to delve into sensationalism, merely for the sake of being sensational, though I could have done this in a number of instances. My purpose has been to show you that God cares for His own. That, should you ever be called upon to face great testings, He is the all sufficient one! Certainly it is true, as His Word says: *There hath no temptation (testing) taken you but such as is common to man: but God is faithful, who will not suffer you to be tempted above that ye are able; but will with the temptation also make a way to escape, that ye may be able to bear it.*

112

I am one who knows that this is true!

On November 17th, 1948, a large contingent of prisoners left our camp, having been told by the Russian guards that the destination was Germany. The preceding night, the names, number, even the freight car to which each had been assigned, was announced. My name was among those selected to leave!

And, once again, the Lord graciously permitted me to undergo testing.

That evening, I slipped on a small stairway and painfully injured my right foot. My heart cried to the Lord, wondering if once more I was to be left behind. For, almost totally crippled by the injury, I would not even so much as be able to march to the railroad tracks!

In desperation, I went to the camp doctor. He looked at the foot, shook his head, and said, "There is nothing I can do. Perhaps you will just have to remain here, and make room for another prisoner."

Ingeniously, one of my comrades devised a small wooden support for my injured foot, making it possible for me to rest my weight, at least partially, upon it. Together, we went off to one side, and I practiced diligently, trying to walk normally so that if a Russian guard should see me, it would not appear that I had suffered any injury.

That night, I lay awake for a long time. Thinking of home, of my dear wife and children, of food and fellowship and friends. But, most of all, of the great goodness of God to me during these many months.

And then I fell asleep.

But in the morning, when I awakened, my foot was swollen and stiff. I could not possibly stand upon it!

O God! I cried out silently. *Why? Why? Why? You know, Lord, that I cannot remain here much longer and live!*

And then, as so often before, I was ashamed. I could trust Him. If He wanted me to go home to the loved ones I so longed to rejoin, He would provide a way.

And He did!

One of my comrades came to me, exclaiming, "They will

be lining up soon to march to the train. But I am working with a detail which is taking food for us to eat on the way. Come quickly, and you can ride!"

With his help I hobbled out of the barracks and over to the kitchen. There stood a small truck, partly loaded. I got on board, and my gracious benefactor covered me with pots and pans.

Here I lay for several hours, scarcely daring to move. At last fully loaded, the truck began to move.

A Russian guard rode at the front of the truck, which had an open cab, and I thought surely I would be apprehended. Once the German POW who sat beside him looked back. Seeing me, he appeared startled for a moment, and I held a finger to my mouth, begging him with my eyes to keep silent.

Does God take care of His own? He certainly does! We stopped alongside the long freight train, directly adjacent to the freight car into which I had been assigned!

I was able to slip out unseen and to get into the freight car. Then, later that afternoon, the remainder of my comrades came. Since, of course, I had not answered roll call at the camp, it was assumed that I would not be going. And so, for seven days as we travelled, I remained huddled completely quiet in my car.

But there was no incident. Although we left our camp on November 17th, and did not arrive at Frankfurt-un-der-Oder until February 28th, just short of three years following my capture, there was no difficulty. Praise be to God!

During these many days of travel, we had better food than we had ever eaten during our entire imprisonment. Only forty eight men were assigned to each car, and there was reasonable warmth. Now and then we would stop, dig our way through the snow to some village where we would get new supplies of food stuffs, but we continued constantly onward until we reached the German border.

Many of the men had died, even on the train as we made

our way home, and so my heart was the more grateful to the Lord for His goodness!

We were met at Frankfurt-un-der-Oder by several pastors, YMCA and Salvation Army representatives. We joined with them in singing "Now Thank We All Our God" and "Praise To The Lord."

I was moved onward immediately, through Eastern Germany into the Western sector. Here I was examined by a doctor and, because of my acute physical condition, sent immediately to the hospital. But not before I had had an opportunity to send a telegram to my wife telling her of my arrival in Germany!

My wife came immediately to the hospital, and such a wonderful reunion!

33

The years have gone now, but not the memories. Even yet, I awaken from dreams of lying in the prison camp. And, very frankly, I do not mind those dreams — though some of them are tinged with horrors which I have not even related to you in this my story — for awakening always brings upon me an overwhelming sense of gratitude to God for His greatness in looking after the needs of one of the least of His children.

Yes, there is gratitude in my heart.

But, my dear Christian friend, there is more than gratitude. There is that for which I shall never cease to thank my God, even throughout the long reaches of eternity. There is within my heart no hatred, not so much as resentment, to the Russians. I can say in complete honesty that I wish every Russian guard I ever met could sit at my table.

I pray for those prison guards! I pray for the civilians I

met! I pray for all the people of Russia! Do you? Certainly no people of earth need the prayers of God's children more than the people of Russia. For they are caught in the spiritual flotsam of the power of the very anti-Christ!

I pray especially for the Christians of Russia, for those who — at the peril of their own mortal existence — are *holding forth the Word of Life!*

True, it is a blessing to live in a land where there is the preaching of the Word of God. It is good to come under the hearing of the Gospel. But be honest, my dear Christian friend, is it not true that the Church of Jesus Christ has lost the real technique of propagating the Gospel — namely that of personal witness?

In Russia, there is little propagation of the Word of God beyond that of personal witness. And I sometimes wonder if, perchance, it could not be that the Church of Jesus Christ is more virulent behind the Iron Curtain than beyond it! For this is why we are upon earth, my Christian brother! We are here to bear witness to the miracle of salvation in our own lives!

Yes, we of the free world have our fine churches, our freedom of worship. But unless we bear bold witness of our faith, to what avail are our churches and our freedom?

I implore you to ask of God for a new love in your heart for those who do not know Him — be they friend or enemy! This is a world that has gone mad over the power of men. World War II was like a breath of hell upon the earth. I know, for I went through it. But man prepares even greater means of destruction. And, unbelievable though it may seem, the Soviet Union — whom even we in Germany considered to be hopelessly backward prior to World War II — rapidly forges to the front in scientific and military achievements.

But there is a greater power than that which can be fashioned by men's hands. There is a power that can only be known by the man upon his knees — the power of the Holy Spirit working through human instruments who proclaim, by living witness, the truth that God loved every man, woman

116

and child upon the earth so much *He gave His only begotten Son, that whosoever believeth in Him should not perish, but have everlasting life. For God sent not His Son into the world to condemn the world; but that the world through Him might be saved.*